THE FACTS ABOUT

TEENAGE
PREGNANCIES

BILL GILLHAM

CASSELL

Cassell
Wellington House
125 Strand
London WC2R 0BB

PO Box 605
Herndon
Virginia 20172

First published 1997

British Library Cataloguing-in-Publication Data
A catalogue record for this book is available from the British Library.

ISBN 0-304-33615-7 (paperback)
ISBN 0-304-33614-9 (hardback)

Typeset by Kenneth Burnley in Irby, Wirral, Cheshire.
Printed and bound in Great Britain by Redwood Books, Trowbridge, Wiltshire

CONTENTS

Series Foreword   ix
Acknowledgements   x

1 The Scale of Teenage Pregnancy   1
   The facts of the matter   1
   Trends in abortion   3
   Births outside marriage   4
   Trends in child-bearing   6
   Social disadvantage and teenage pregnancy   7

2 Teenage Pregnancy: Context and Consequences   10
   Is it a problem?   10
   The rise of the lone-parent and unmarried family 12
   The family background of teenage mothers   13
   Medical risks associated with teenage pregnancy 14
   Mortality rates for babies born to teenage mothers 15
   'Cot death', other 'undetermined' deaths, and
      social and marital status   17
   Teenage mothers and Sudden Infant Death Syndrome 18
   Teenage maternity, infanticide and 'suspicious' deaths 20
   Teenage parents, child abuse and neglect   21
   Lone parents, child abuse and neglect   22
   Maternal age and child abuse   22
   Social support and maternal depression   23
   Conclusion   24

3 Teenage Sexual Behaviour   27
   The opposition to research   27
   Sex and society   29
   Adolescent sexual behaviour   29
   Age at first intercourse   30

Contents

Why has age at first intercourse declined? 32

Social class 33

Educational level 34

Ethnic and religious group membership 34

The experience of first intercourse 35

Age of partner at first intercourse 35

The issue of exploitation 36

'Unplanned' sexual activity 36

The romantic view of sex 37

4 Sex Education 38

The background 38

Why sex education? 38

Is school the main source of information? 39

Sex education in schools 40

Education and sexual behaviour 41

Changing knowledge and changing behaviour 42

'Rationality' and 'decisions' about sexual behaviour 43

Teenage pregnancy: the lessons from international
comparisons 44

Specific programme evaluations 46

Four programmes that worked 46

Conclusion 48

5 Contraception and Abortion 49

The current reality 49

Abortion and contraceptive failure 50

A glimpse at history 51

Contraceptive use by teenagers 52

Contraceptive use by marital status 54

Contraceptive use and teenage sexual behaviour 55

Teenage reluctance to use contraceptive services 56

Improving the situation 57

Contents

6 Policy and Practice   59

   Government policy   59

   What is the problem?   60

   The moral objections to teenage pregnancy   62

   The politics of choice   63

   Poverty and social disadvantage   64

   Improvement of educational standards and
      employment prospects for young people   64

   Improving the adequacy of sex education   65

   Improving confidence in GPs and access to
      contraceptive services   66

   Moral ambivalence about adolescent sexuality   68

References   69

Appendix A   77

   Useful addresses and telephone numbers

   Agencies concerned with parenthood, contraception
     and sex education

Appendix B   80

   Recommended publications for professionals,
     parents, teenagers and children

Index   83

SERIES FOREWORD

The idea for this series came from an awareness that much of the media hype, and some of the professional practice, relating to major social problems involving children and adolescents was singularly ill-informed. At the same time there was a notable lack of short, accessible summaries of the relevant research data by which people could inform themselves.

Not surprisingly, the conclusions that are drawn from a careful consideration of the evidence challenge many generally held assumptions – at all levels of popular and professional concern.

Bill Gillham

ACKNOWLEDGEMENTS

Jane Cuthill word-processed successive drafts at speed; Judith Gillham checked corrections and, as always, improved the style. I am grateful to both for this indispensable help. The following have given permission to reproduce copyright figures and tables: Yale University Press and the Alan Guttmacher Institute for Figure 1.1, Figure 4.1; The Family Policy Studies Centre and the Joseph Rowntree Foundation for Figure 1.2, Figure 1.3, Table 1.1, Figure 1.4; HMSO for Table 1.2, Figure 2.1, Table 2.7, Table 5.1; The Registrar General for Scotland for Figure 1.5, Figure 2.2; The British Medical Association for Table 1.4, Table 1.5; Susan Creighton and the NSPCC for Table 2.6; A. M. Johnson, J. Wadsworth, K. Wellings, J. Field and Blackwell Scientific Publications for Table 3.2, Figure 3.1, Table 3.3, Table 3.4, Table 5.2, Table 5.3. Specific publication sources are given in the text. The re-analysis of published statistics on post-neonatal death reported in Chapter 2 was carried out as part of a research project on infant death funded by the Nuffield Foundation; Suzanne Mackinnon, as research assistant, was involved in this. Suzanne's help and the support of the Foundation are gratefully acknowledged.

1

THE SCALE OF TEENAGE PREGNANCY

THE FACTS OF THE MATTER

Teenage pregnancy is nothing new, and the popular perception that there is an ever-increasing number of such pregnancies is incorrect. There were 10,000 *fewer* maternities (live births) to teenage mothers in 1991 than in 1981, and 42,000 fewer than in 1971 (Burghes and Brown, 1995, p. 14). Births to teenagers were at their peak in the 1960s as the following graph shows:

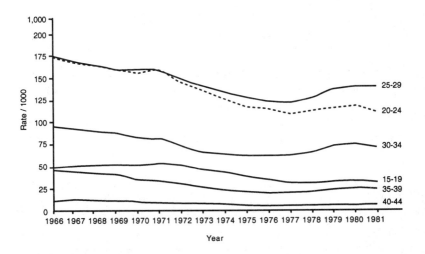

Figure 1.1. Births per 1,000 women, by age group, 1966–81. (Jones *et al.*, 1986, p. 96.)

It is, of course, necessary to make a distinction between *conception* rates and *birth* rates: over the past 25 years abortion has become a major factor in the equation (see Chapter 5). We can see the scale of that influence by looking at recent maternity and conception rates. Figure 1.2 shows the figures for *numbers* of teenage conceptions and maternities.

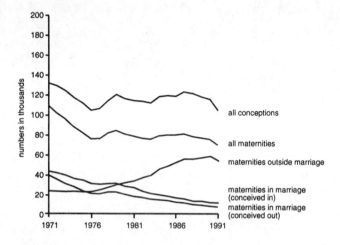

Figure 1.2. Trends in maternities for women who conceived as teenagers: total numbers England and Wales, 1971–91. (Burghes and Brown, *op. cit.,* p. 14.)

It can be seen that after a drop in the mid-1970s there was an erratic tendency for conceptions to increase from the latter part of that decade onwards – interestingly as economic conditions worsened. From the beginning of the 1990s there is again a downward trend and *this has continued* (Brook Advisory Centre Annual Report, 1996a). The gap between 'all conceptions' and 'all maternities' reflects the abortion factor and we need to look at this more closely by examining *rates* rather than absolute *numbers*. The following graph (Figure 1.3) comes from a report by the Family Policy Studies Centre (1995) based on data by Babb (1993): it shows conception rates by *outcome* for women under 20 from 1971 to 1991.

Legal abortion has been available in the UK since 1967 and has rapidly become established as a major factor in the birth rate *at all ages*. It can easily be seen from Figure 1.3 that the gap between conceptions and maternities has steadily widened as a result of the termination of pregnancies.

2

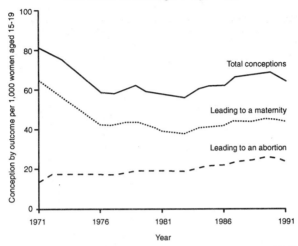

Figure 1.3. Conception rates by outcome for women aged under 20, England and Wales, 1971–91

TRENDS IN ABORTION

Few people realize how commonplace abortion has become. Currently around a quarter of *all* pregnancies (inside and outside marriage) are terminated. About a third of pregnancies outside marriage are terminated. The implications of this are discussed in Chapter 5 but the situation is a serious one, irrespective of the ethical issues, because of the largely unknown physical and psychological consequences for women – and the enormous economic cost to the NHS.

Table 1.1 shows the percentage outcomes for women at all ages for conceptions *outside* marriage, i.e. birth outside marriage, birth inside marriage, or termination.

In general the abortion rate has declined since 1990 when the rate was 13.6 per 1,000 women; by 1994 the rate had fallen to 12.2. Abortion is, however, increasingly a service for unmarried women. Table 1.2 (see page 5) shows the number of abortions in England and Wales by age and marital status for 1994.

It can be seen that *two-thirds* of all abortions are to unmarried women, though only a quarter of these are teenagers. It is not until the age of 30-plus that abortions to married women come into the majority. That is the present situation; we need now to look at the

Table 1.1. Conceptions outside and inside marriage. Outcomes as a proportion of conceptions by age level: England and Wales, 1971, 1981, 1991. (Burghes and Brown, 1995, p. 12.)

	1971 (%)			1981 (%)			1991 (%)		
	Outside	Inside	Termin-ation	Outside	Inside	Termin-ation	Outside	Inside	Termin-ation
All ages	34	36	30	41	19	40	57	9	34
Under 16	44	19	37	38	5	57	48	1	51
Under 20	29	45	26	39	20	41	57	5	38
20–24	33	34	33	41	20	39	57	9	35
25–29	44	22	34	44	18	36	58	10	31
30–34	49	17	34	42	19	39	59	11	30
35–39	50	13	38	39	13	49	55	11	34
Over 40	48	12	40	30	8	63	43	7	50

trends over the past 25 years which have radically altered the relationship between marriage and maternities, and which lie at the heart of what is perceived to be the problem of teenage pregnancy.

BIRTHS OUTSIDE MARRIAGE

In 1971 most teenage conceptions resulted in a birth within marriage; by 1991 only about a sixth resulted in marriage by the time of birth. Not all of these are 'lone' mothers. Of the births that took place outside marriage in 1994, for example, the majority (66.6 per cent) were registered by both parents of whom more than half (59.2 per cent) were living at the same address, and presumably cohabiting. 33.4 per cent of births outside marriage to teenagers were registered solely by the mother, compared with 71 per cent in 1971 (ONS, 1996b). The general picture is that in 1971 only around 10 per cent of births occurred outside marriage. The figure now is more than three times that. Figure 1.4 represents that change graphically.

The steep increase dates from the mid-1970s. 'Rates' and percentages are only part of the story and the figures for different age levels show a major demographic trend. *At all ages many more babies are being born outside marriage.* Indeed, over the past decade or so the biggest changes have occurred to women in their twenties. Table 1.3 illustrates this.

Note that at *all* age levels more babies are being born outside marriage and that the smallest increase over that decade (in percentage and number) is amongst teenagers. Note also that *fewer*

Table 1.2. Numbers of legal abortions by age and marital status: England and Wales, 1994. (ONS, 1996a.)

Marital status	All ages	Under 15	15	16–19	20–24	25–29	30–34	35–39	40–44	45 and over	Not stated
Total	**156,539**	**1,080**	**2,166**	**25,223**	**44,871**	**38,081**	**25,507**	**14,156**	**5,008**	**440**	**7**
Single	102,532	1,080	2,166	24,219	38,108	23,482	9,585	3,152	685	53	2
Married	34,632	–	–	325	3,814	9,159	10,620	7,460	2,968	283	3
Separated	5,928	–	–	56	834	1,893	1,804	1,013	309	19	–
Divorced	7,344	–	–	42	554	1,820	2,323	1,784	765	55	1
Widowed	449	–	–	3	33	92	114	131	65	11	–
Not stated	5,654	–	–	578	1,528	1,635	1,061	616	216	19	1

Table 1.3. Live births within and outside marriage, by age level, England and Wales, 1984 and 1994. Numbers are given in rounded thousands. (ONS, 1996b)

Year	Under 20		20–24		25–29		30–34		35–39	
	Marriage Within	Outside	Marriage Within	Outside	Marriage Within	Outside	Marriage Within	Outside	Marriage Within	Outside
1984	21	33	150	41	197	21	113	10	38	5
1994	7	36	69	71	171	58	146	34	50	13

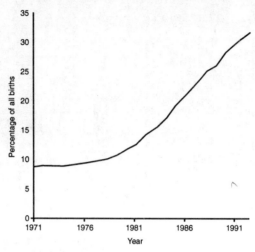

Figure 1.4. Births outside marriage as a percentage of all births: England and Wales, 1971–91. (FPSC, 1995, p. 8, Fig. 13.)

babies are being born to women in their early twenties and more babies are being born to women in their thirties. This represents a major demographic trend: part of the shifting picture that puts teenage motherhood in an increasingly distinct category.

TRENDS IN CHILD-BEARING

A typical picture of long-term changing trends is shown in Figure 1.5 which illustrates live birth rates in Scotland, by age of mother, for the 35-year period from 1961 to 1995.

The pattern reflected here is general throughout the UK. Note the following:

- teenage maternities have been *relatively* steady since the mid-1970s and are not radically different from the early 1960s;
- over the same period (mid-1970s onward) an increase in rates is apparent for women aged 35–39 and particularly those aged 30–34;
- rates for women in this latter category have overtaken those for women aged 20–24 since the early 1990s;
- the age range 20–24 is the one which has seen the most rapid decline in the birth rate (and, as we saw earlier, this is the age range where the *number* of abortions is highest).

6

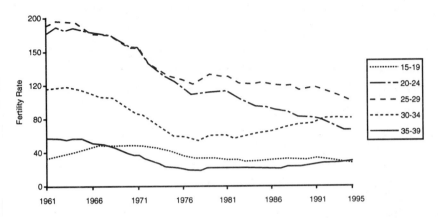

Figure 1.5. Live births per 1,000 women, by age of mother, Scotland, 1961–95. (GRO, 1996, p. 29, Fig. 3.1.)

SOCIAL DISADVANTAGE AND TEENAGE PREGNANCY

Data on this important issue are hard to locate, largely because it does not form part of national level official statistics which, necessarily, rely upon official records, e.g. birth registration and the like.

In any case, social disadvantage has a peculiarly *local* character: in large urban areas relating not just to occupation and income but also area of residence. The three are, of course, highly correlated. Smith (1993) carried out a detailed analysis, along these lines, of teenage pregnancies in the Tayside area of Scotland, concentrating in particular on pregnancies in girls under 16.

Local areas of residence were graded from 7 (the most deprived) to 1 (the most affluent) using the categories devised by Carstairs and Morris (1991) based on four variables derived from 1981 census data (per cent male unemployment; per cent social classes IV and V; per cent without car; per cent overcrowded housing).

Table 1.4 shows the pregnancy rates from this study in young women aged 15–19, by deprivation category for the period 1980 to 1990.

The figures over the decade are remarkably consistent in showing that young women in the most deprived areas are between four and eight times more likely to become pregnant as teenagers than

Table 1.4. Average annual rate of pregnancies per 1000 girls aged 15–19 by socioeconomic conditions in area of residence: Tayside 1980 to 1990. (Data from Smith, 1993, p. 1234.)

Deprivation category	Annual average rate per 1,000 girls aged 15 to 19			
	1980–82	*1983–85*	*1986–88*	*1989–90*
7	128	124	185	135
6	80	75	106	103
5	70	73	88	83
4	50	52	58	57
3	42	40	45	49
2	35	32	32	32
1	21	30	22	23

7 = most deprived; 1 = most affluent

those in the most affluent areas. The implication is that social factors have a major impact on sexual behaviour and that teenage pregnancies have to be seen as endemic in some areas, largely because of broad social conditions.

The answer is unlikely to lie just (or even mainly) in the provision of better contraceptive and abortion services. As Smith (*op. cit.*) goes on to demonstrate, abortion is least likely to be resorted to by those groups who are most likely to become pregnant:

Table 1.5. Legal abortions as a percentage of total teenage pregnancies: Tayside 1980–90

Deprivation category	*1980–82*	*1983–85*	*1986–88*	*1989–90*
7	27.2	24.8	23.9	29.1
6	36.3	32.3	28.3	33.3
5	28.9	32.4	32.1	41.3
4	40.0	41.9	37.6	41.3
3	45.8	44.7	47.6	47.8
2	47.7	47.4	49.8	54.0
1	64.1	66.0	60.6	62.2

7 = most deprived; 1 = most affluent

Young women in the most affluent groups (the least vulnerable section) are two to three times more likely to obtain a termination. This is not linked to cost or the availability of such services.

A much larger-scale (but more coarse-grained) study of the English regions by Wilson, Brown and Richards (1992) also found that teenage abortion rates were highest in the most affluent areas, i.e. the south and south-east, again irrespective of provision. They comment: 'Girls who conceive as teenagers seem to be the very girls who would find contraception difficult to use – they are under-achievers at school, and are from socially deprived and often large families' (p. 23). They conclude:

> The problem is not so easily solved and the possible solution may be beyond the control of the health services . . . . Reduction of the social factors which precipitate teenage conception may have more impact than a re-investment in traditional family planning services. (p. 23)

As we shall see in Chapter 5, contraceptive services need to break out of the 'family planning' mould if they are to operate as an effective pregnancy prevention service for teenagers. But as indicated by the authors just cited, a 'contraceptive service' view of the problem may be too narrow. Teenage pregnancy has to be seen as part of a system of interlocking (and largely disadvantaging) factors. We need to look at the context in which it occurs.

2

TEENAGE PREGNANCY: CONTEXT AND CONSEQUENCES

IS IT A PROBLEM?

Whether something is seen as a problem or not depends on how you 'construct' it – the attitudes and values that define your perspective. For many women who are determined on a career, pregnancy before their late twenties would be seen as a personal and professional disaster; for them, that is.

The statistical data summarized in the previous chapter could be seen in these terms; but such data are neutral and, in any case, need to be given the human, qualitative dimension. When we do this the 'problem' changes character or, at the very least, suggests different interpretations.

The authors of a recent review of teenage pregnancy in the UK in the 1990s point out that:

> At the heart of intentions to change the rate of teenage pregnancy lies the simple assumption that each pregnancy is bad for everyone; the girl, her family, the health services, the education authorities and society in general. Thus teenage pregnancy is perceived as a disaster for all concerned. (Jacobson, Wilkinson and Pill, 1995, p. 233)

There is a significant amount of evidence that many teenagers are happy to find themselves pregnant. A US study from the mid-1970s found that 23 per cent of the sample intended to become pregnant (Shah, Zelnik and Kantner, 1975). And a more recent UK study (Simms and Smith, 1986) put the figure nearer 40 per cent. This latter report entitled 'Teenage mothers and their partners' is recommended reading as an insight into a situation which is easily over-simplified by those whose lives and values are remote from it. For example, the authors of this study report that: 'Despite, or perhaps even because they tended to come from rather deprived backgrounds and to have had rather restricted lives, the majority of teenage mothers in our sample were delighted with their babies and their way of life and would not have had it otherwise' (pp. 8–9). A total of 533 teenage mothers were interviewed nationally in the study, initially when their babies were two to four months old; 89 per cent of the mothers were re-interviewed a year later. The initial assessment found that:

- nine out of ten of the young mothers described their health as 'good' since having the baby;
- four out of five said they did not go short of anything they needed;
- a similar proportion thought they were at least as well off as their contemporaries who did not have children;
- three-quarters thought their job prospects had not been affected;
- two-thirds thought their housing was suitable for their present needs;
- a similar proportion thought things had worked out better than they had expected;
- nine out of ten thought things were going well for them and there was little they wanted to change;
- three-quarters were certain they wanted further children.

At follow-up a year later, the picture was rather less rosy and there was a general sense that their situation was seen as more difficult, but nine out of ten still said that, on balance, they were pleased they had had their baby when they did.

The positive emphasis this chapter begins with is partly to signal the need to avoid a pre-emptive value judgement and partly to emphasize that the experiences reported are *despite* the apparently or supposedly adverse conditions that young, and usually unmarried, mothers have to contend with. We have to consider also whether teenage pregnancy is *intrinsically* a bad thing or whether some of the apparent consequences are due to the difficulties the young mothers have to contend with – particularly their economic circumstances. We start with family structure and income.

11

THE RISE OF THE LONE-PARENT AND UNMARRIED FAMILY

Figure 2.1 shows the percentage of families headed by a lone parent in Great Britain from 1971 to 1993. If it is possible for a graph to be eloquent this is it.

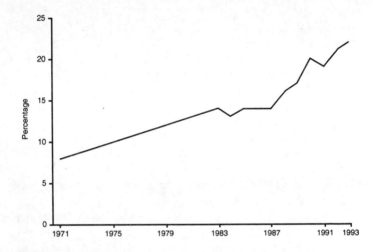

Figure 2.1. Percentage of families headed by a lone parent: Great Britain, 1971–93. (OPCS, 1995b.)

The proportion of families headed by a lone parent increased from 8 per cent in 1971 to 22 per cent in 1993. The biggest increase was in single, i.e. unmarried mother, households (1 per cent in 1971 to 8 per cent in 1993); over the same period households headed by a divorced mother increased from 2 per cent to 7 per cent. The proportion of lone-father families has hardly varied (1–2 per cent) since 1971. Teenage mothers have been largely responsible for the rise in the 'single mother' category. The poverty of this group is striking.

Table 2.1 shows the *extreme* categories of gross weekly household income by family type for Great Britain in 1993

Table 2.1. Usual gross weekly income for married couples, all lone mothers, and single mothers: percentages in highest and lowest categories: Great Britain, 1993. (OPCS, 1995b.)

Family type	Income up to £100 per week	Income above £350 per week
Married couple	5%	56%
All lone mothers	46%	9%
Single mothers	60%	6%

The inverse relationship is striking: many of the 'consequences' of being a single mother (teenage or not) could be accounted for simply in terms of poverty. Indeed, given the extreme nature of the data, one can only wonder that things are not much worse. It is, perhaps, testimony to the resilience of women in general, and young women in particular.

THE FAMILY BACKGROUND OF TEENAGE MOTHERS

Simms and Smith (*op. cit.*) in their in-depth study of teenage mothers identified a number of distinguishing features which have implications for the personal and economic support of teenage mothers by their families. In summary:

- the young women were predominantly (81 per cent) from working-class homes – compared with fewer than 60 per cent in the national pattern;
- they tended to come from large families – average size 4.4 children – more than twice the national average;
- one-third came from a broken home (41 per cent in the case of *single* teenage mothers);
- nearly a third (29 per cent) of the teenage mothers had mothers who themselves had started having children before the age of 20.

It can be seen that there are positive as well as negative elements here. Grandmothers who were similarly placed themselves are likely to view their daughter's pregnancy as more normal and less of a disaster than families with a different tradition of child-bearing. In particular there may be less pressure for abortion – a factor

13

which Smith (1993, p. 1235) marks as a particular matter of concern in the case of teenage conceptions in the more affluent social classes.

In all that follows about the specific risks of teenage pregnancies the range of relevant social and socio-economic factors must be borne in mind. As we shall see, they are so closely interwoven that disentangling them is a tricky exercise in research methodology.

MEDICAL RISKS ASSOCIATED WITH TEENAGE PREGNANCY

In general the risks are highest for the youngest teenagers. For example, maternal mortality, which is comparatively rare in the present day, occurs at the rate of one per thousand young mothers under the age of 16 – ten times the rate for those aged 16–29 and as high as for maternities to women in their mid-forties (Beard, 1981).

Specific risks related directly to pregnancy are increased rates for:

- hypertension (high blood pressure);
- anaemia;
- pre-eclampsia. (Russel, 1988)

This last is a serious condition involving a number of factors (hypertension and malfunctioning of the kidneys) and can be life-threatening.

Risks more directly affecting the baby are:

- prematurity;
- 'low birth-weight for dates', i.e. small but not premature;
- increased rates for perinatal and neonatal mortality.

There is also a much increased rate, compared with older, and especially *married* mothers – of post-neonatal mortality – in partic-ular 'cot death' (sudden infant death syndrome). However, social/care factors are implicated here and are discussed below.

A recent large-scale study in the US (Fraser, Brockert and Ward, 1995) has gone some way to teasing out the role of *biological* imma-turity in these medical disadvantages of teenage pregnancy, independent of socio-economic disadvantages. The authors analysed data for some 134,000 white first-born infants between

1970 and 1990 whose mothers were 13 to 24 years of age. Low birth weight and prematurity in those aged 13–17 was almost twice the rate for mothers aged 20–24. Moreover, these risks remained significantly greater even amongst those teenagers who were married, had an appropriate level of education and had received adequate prenatal care. Because these authors were careful to control for the influence of socio-economic factors, their finding that there is some independent risk (for babies born to teenage mothers) is of importance.

MORTALITY RATES FOR BABIES BORN TO TEENAGE MOTHERS

Probably no other single index reflects variations in social conditions between countries (and within them) as the infant mortality rate – the death rate during the first year amongst babies born alive. In the mid-1990s the rate was 6.2 per 1,000 in England and Wales and Scotland, 3.4 in Sweden, 8.3 in the USA, 6.4 in France and so on. Rates are much higher in former Eastern Block countries – 23.3 in Romania, for example (GRO, 1996, p. 12).

So much for present-day international comparisons. Within the UK (as elsewhere) infant mortality rates have dropped dramatically in recent times. In Scotland, where longitudinal data are routinely published, the rate for 1946–50 was 47.3 per 1,000 – almost five per cent. By 1995 it had fallen to 0.62 per cent. Not least impressive is the fact that much of the improvement has occurred in the last 25 years (GRO, 1996).

Figure 2.2 shows neonatal, post-neonatal and infant death rates per 1,000 live births in Scotland from 1971 to 1995. The 'infant death' category is the sum of neonatal deaths (under four weeks) and post-neonatal deaths (over four weeks but under twelve months).

Social class differences in infant death rates are now very much less than they were, although infant deaths in the lowest category V (unskilled manual) are still almost 50 per cent higher than the rate for babies born to parents in the 'non-manual' categories (GRO, 1996, p. 51; ONS, 1996c, p. 226). These data relate to married parents. Social class (by father's occupation) is generally given in official statistics only for *married* parents, but approximately one-third of babies are born to *unmarried* parents. It is here that infant death is particularly high – accounting for two-fifths of the total

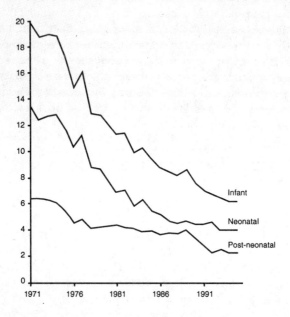

Figure 2.2. Neonatal, post-neonatal and infant death rates per 1,000 live births: Scotland 1971–95. (GRO, 1996, p. 4, Fig. 4.2.)

(GRO, 1996, p. 52; ONS, 1996c, p. 221). Most teenage parents are in this category.

In England and Wales (ONS, 1996c) data on infant deaths now distinguish between children born inside marriage, those born outside marriage but *jointly* registered (and whether the parents have the same or different addresses) and those registered solely by the mother. In the 'outside marriage' groups rates are highest for those births jointly registered, but where the parents have different addresses, and those registered by the mother alone. However the most marked difference is for social class within the 'jointly registered' group. Here infant deaths in the lowest category V (unskilled manual) are at least twice the rate for the highest category I (professional/managerial); and the rate for the 'unclassified' category – presumably those unemployed – is *three times* as great.

Clearly being unmarried at the top end of the social scale means something quite different from the lower end. *Maternal age* appears to be the main factor in the equation, since, amongst older women, this social class differential is largely reduced (ONS, 1996c, pp. 226–27).

Simms and Smith (1986) in the study previously cited found that at the time they revisited their sample of teenage mothers a year later, four per cent of the babies had died – an extremely high rate, twice the national average of two per cent for teenage mothers: a rate which is itself three times greater than the national average for *all* births.

The reasons behind this high rate are not clear but they are likely to be social rather than purely medical. And they have to be seen in the context of historical trends and the international comparisons cited earlier. By that standard alone teenage mothers are shown as a seriously disadvantaged group. Table 2.2 shows infant mortality rates for mothers of different ages in England and Wales, 1994 .

Table 2.2. Infant mortality rates per 1,000 live births by maternal age: England and Wales, 1992 . (ONS, 1996c, p. 221,, Table 19.)

Under 20	20–24	25–29	30–34	35+
9.8	7.3	5.3	5.3	6.3

This table gives a gross comparison by age. We need to look at this more closely so as to see what kind of causes contribute to the high infant mortality rate for teenage mothers.

'COT DEATH', OTHER 'UNDETERMINED' DEATHS, AND SOCIAL AND MARITAL STATUS

Childhood mortality statistics for England and Wales are now published by the Office for National Statistics (ONS) – formerly the Office of Population Census and Surveys (OPCS), and for Scotland by the General Register Office (GRO). These reports classify the causes of death in accordance with the International Statistical Classification of Diseases, Injuries and Causes of Death (ICD), the Ninth Revision of which has operated by international agreement since January 1979. Each 'cause' has its own ICD number and these have to be used on official death certificates. In theory this standardization allows for international comparison of rates for different causes of death. In practice, different professional procedures and legal systems can mean that deaths are entered in one category in preference to another, though the precise reasons are not usually clear. This is particularly apparent in the case of infant death where definite causes or circumstances may be hard to determine.

Two categories of infant death are particularly liable to this kind of variation. These are:

- sudden death in infancy syndrome – popularly known as 'cot death' – ICD 798;
- injury 'undetermined whether accidentally or purposely inflicted' – ICD E980–E989.

TEENAGE MOTHERS AND SUDDEN INFANT DEATH SYNDROME

As recently as 1988 SIDS accounted for 50 per cent of all post-neonatal deaths in England and Wales. There has been a dramatic decline since then – to just under 27 per cent in 1994 – presumably due to the widely disseminated advice that babies should be put to sleep on their backs, not 'overheated', and that parents should avoid smoking, etc. (ONS, 1996c). However, it is likely that medical practitioners are also using the 'diagnosis' more conservatively because of increased awareness of its limitations.

Sudden Infant Death Syndrome is defined as 'the death, unexpected by history, of any infant or young child in whom a thorough post-mortem examination fails to show an adequate cause' (cited by Berger, 1979, p. 554). It is therefore a *negative* diagnosis where a cause cannot, in fact, be established. The diagnosis of SIDS, often described as 'cot death', carries with it connotations of unexplained *natural* causes. The notion that a proportion of such deaths may be due to neglect or abuse is only slowly gaining recognition (see review in Gillham, 1994, pp. 63–67). Suffice it to say here that SIDS, unlike most other causes of infant death, shows a marked variation according to the social situation of the parents (i.e. poor, unmarried, young, with a history of criminality or abuse). For example, Newlands and Emery (1991) found that the SIDS rate amongst the siblings of children on the Child Abuse Register was *five times* the rate for the population as a whole. A study by Pugh, Statham and Jarvis (1987) found a rate nine times the national average amongst mothers who were on probation.

If we look at the national picture we find that the Sudden Infant Death rates for babies born to teenage mothers are four to eleven times higher than mothers in the 25-plus categories. Table 2.3 gives the precise data.

Table 2.3. Sudden infant death rates per 1,000 live births by maternal age: England and Wales, 1995. (ONS, 1996d.)

Under 20	*20–24*	*25–29*	*30–34*	*35–39*	*40+*
2.08	1.00	0.46	0.27	0.43	0.18

What this means is that one baby in 500 born to a teenage mother is likely to suffer a 'cot death', compared to one in 3,000–5,000 to mothers over 30: this difference is so extreme that social, rather than 'medical' causes are indicated.

A further light is cast on the situation if we look at SIDS deaths according to marital status, i.e. born to married or unmarried parents. As we saw in Chapter 1 this latter category is more often poor; and most teenage mothers are unmarried.

Table 2.4 shows the numbers and rates of SIDS deaths amongst babies born to married and unmarried parents in England and Wales during 1995.

Table 2.4. Sudden infant deaths: numbers and rates per 1,000 live births, by marital status: England and Wales, 1995. (ONS, 1996d.)

	Marital status	
	Married	*Unmarried*
Numbers	138	258
Rates	0.32	1.17

Note that the absolute *numbers* of such deaths where parents are unmarried is almost double the number where parents are married, even though only about 35 per cent of babies are born to unmarried parents. Overall this is a pattern of infant death which reflects social disadvantage; but the precise causes are not clear or certain.

TEENAGE MATERNITY, INFANTICIDE AND 'SUSPICIOUS' DEATHS

Infant deaths due to 'external' causes: accidents (fire, suffocation, drowning, head injuries); murder, and 'injuries undetermined whether accidentally or purposely caused' are significantly higher amongst the babies of teenage mothers. Table 2.5 gives numbers and rates for post-neonatal deaths by maternal age for England and Wales 1992 (note that these data are not given in the 1996 publication for the years 1993 and 1994).

Table 2.5. Post-neonatal deaths due to 'external causes of injury and poisoning', numbers and rates per 1,000 live births by maternal age. England and Wales, 1992. (OPCS, 1995a.)

	Under 20	20–24	25–29	30–34	35–39
Numbers	16	25	19	11	4
Rates	0.3	0.2	0.1	0.1	0.1

Because rates for teenage mothers are three times greater than for mothers 25-plus, again social rather than medical factors are indicated. Evidence about the causes of infant death is notoriously difficult to obtain – hence the adoption (in 1966) of the 'undetermined category'. The probability that this category does in fact include mainly homicides is underlined by research carried out in the US by Jason, Carpenter and Tyler (1983) and published in a paper entitled 'Under-recording of infant homicide in the United States'. Trends in broad social factors (income, employment, fertility, crime levels) are usually linked to each other in that changes affect *all* ages and classes – whilst maintaining typical differences. In the US, at a time when homicide was generally increasing (1960–76), there was an apparent sudden drop in infant homicides following the introduction of the 'undetermined' category in the 8th Revision of the ICD index in 1966. When the number of infant deaths from this category was added to the established infant homicides, the trend was essentially the same as for other broad age ranges.

It should be noted here that although child murder is uncommon in the UK it is most common in the under-5 age range, with parents normally implicated. For example, in 1994 there were 47 murders of children under 15 years: 32 of these were aged under 5 (ONS, 1996e).

TEENAGE PARENTS, CHILD ABUSE AND NEGLECT

The main source of data on the parental situation of abused and neglected children in England and Wales remains the longitudinal studies carried out by the NSPCC covering a 17-year period up to 1990 (Creighton, 1985; Creighton and Noyes, 1989; Creighton, 1992). Until that date the NSPCC were responsible for maintaining about 10 per cent of the Child Abuse/Protection Registers in the UK. As a 10 per cent sample it has a reasonable chance of providing representative data.

In the final report from that study (Creighton, 1992) the parental situation of physically injured children in the sample was as shown in Table 2.6.

Table 2.6. Parental situation of physically injured children in England and Wales 1988–90 combined: NSSPCC sample

Reason for registration	Parental situation						
	2 NPs No. (%)	NMA No. (%)	NM & Fas No. (%)	NFA No. (%)	NF & MoS No. (%)	Other No. (%)	Total %
Physical Injury	972 (35)	649 (23)	735 (26)	84 (3)	92 (3)	69 (3)	(100)

2NPs	-	Two natural parents
NMA	-	Natural mother alone
NM & FaS	-	Natural mother and father substitute
NFA	-	Natural father alone
NF & MoS	-	Natural father and mother subsitute
Other	-	Includes relatives, foster parents and other parental situations

A figure of 26 per cent of the children living with lone parents looks unremarkable in the late 1990s when the national figure *for all ages* of children is over 20 per cent. However, physically abused children are more likely to be under five years of age (Department of Health, 1996) and a longitudinal follow-up of a national cohort of children, for the same period as the NSPCC study, by Butler and Golding (1986) found that, at that time, over 90 per cent of children aged 5 were living with both natural parents. Using this as a baseline comparison lone parents are clearly more at risk of abusing their children. Why is that?

LONE PARENTS, CHILD ABUSE AND NEGLECT

As we saw earlier in this chapter, lone parenthood is equated with poverty to a remarkable degree; and poverty and child abuse are strongly associated (see review in Gillham, 1994).

Gelles (1989) in a US study following on from a national survey concluded that *poverty* rather than being *lone* explained the higher rate of violence towards children in such families – at least for lone *mothers*; lone fathers were more likely to be violent whatever their income level, but there were fewer of them in the first place. But in society as a whole, the ratio of around 9:1 for lone mothers to lone fathers appears very general. This is a major reason why mothers are as likely as fathers to be implicated in child abuse: their involvement is disproportionate (Creighton, 1992).

MATERNAL AGE AND CHILD ABUSE

Since teenage mothers are very likely to be poor and relatively unsupported (Garbarino, 1976) it is hardly surprising to find a high incidence of abuse and neglect in families headed by young mothers. We shall examine the role of support systems a little later. First we must deal with the 'maternal age' factor.

Holden, Willis and Corcoran (1992) carried out an extensive review of the literature on young maternal age in relation to child abuse and neglect. Their conclusions warrant direct quotation:

> Young maternal age as a predictor of subsequent child
> maltreatment was evaluated in ten separate investiga-
> tions with mixed results. Six of the studies which did not
> support age as a risk factor were generally well-con-
> trolled prospective investigations . . . those four studies
> which found younger mothers to be at great risk for
> subsequent child maltreatment utilized retrospective
> designs . . . In addition, two of these four investigations
> . . . did not control for socio-economic status. When
> researchers controlled for SES in the previously cited
> prospective investigations, age no longer surfaced as
> an important predictive variable. A similar pattern of
> results across investigations was obtained for single
> marital status during pregnancy. (p. 25)

A more recent study by Stier *et al.* (1993) using a longitudinal case-cohort design, i.e. following up groups of mothers over a period of time, and which compared mothers aged 18 and younger with those aged 19–24 in comparable circumstances, did find a rate of maltreatment for the younger mothers twice the rate for older mothers (even when this was restricted to 19–20 year olds). It should be noted, however, that it was not usually the mother who was responsible for the maltreatment.

The ability of young mothers to care for, and protect, their children is dependent on their social and emotional resources. The US study by Garbarino (1976) cited earlier concluded that 'the degree to which mothers are subjected to socio-economic stress *without adequate support systems*, accounts for a substantial proportion of the variance in rates of maltreatment' (p. 607).

SOCIAL SUPPORT AND MATERNAL DEPRESSION

Women are particularly vulnerable to depression, the female/male ratio being at least 2:1 (Paykel, 1991). How far this is biologically determined it is impossible to say because of the extent to which social roles, and acceptable ways of showing distress, are culturally determined.

What is clear is that the social circumstances of women account for a large variation in the incidence of clinical, as well as more mild forms of depression. The key study in this area: *Social Origins of Depression: A Study of Psychiatric Disorder in Women* (Brown and Harris, 1978) has not had its main findings modified by subsequent research (Paykel, *op. cit.*). By pointing to the social correlates of serious depression in women, Brown and Harris shifted the emphasis away from 'personality' explanations onto the risk-increasing and risk-reducing factors in the social environment. These are of particular relevance to teenage mothers. At the same time it must be said that relative youth in itself seems to confer some degree of immunity: depression peaks in older women, particularly as they approach middle age (Paykel, *op. cit.*).

In depression there is usually a *precipitating event*, a stressful life experience which acts as 'the last straw'. Whether a woman becomes depressed depends upon a number of risk-increasing factors:

- low social class/educational standard;
- lack of intimate support (not necessarily from a 'partner');
- early loss of mother;
- young children;
- lack of employment.

Brown and Harris found these factors to be *cumulative*, i.e. the more adverse factors, the more likely women were to become depressed.

We have to be cautious about generalizing these findings about women in general to teenage mothers. However, Wolkind and Kruk (1985), in a UK study of pregnant teenagers and motherhood, found that those who had support from their families and friends were less prone to depression than those who lacked such support. The study of Simms and Smith (1986) cited earlier provides data on the prevalence of depression in this group. They were able to follow up 456 teenage mothers from their initial sample approximately one year later. Just over two-fifths of the women reported that they had suffered from 'depression or nerves' in the intervening period. Of course, this does not amount to a clinical diagnosis of depression, but it is an index of psychological distress. The factors in the young women's lives which were associated with this kind of distress are given in Table 2.7 (from Simms and Smith, *op. cit.*, p. 69). It can be seen that the picture is essentially similar to that found by Brown and Harris.

Apart from the unhappiness experienced by the young women themselves, a depressed mother is also an inadequate one as far as the baby is concerned.

A prospective longitudinal study of mothers considered at risk for abuse and neglect – the Minnesota mother-child interaction project (Farber and Egeland, 1987) – examined specifically the effects on their children of a group of depressed and withdrawn women. They called these the 'psychologically unavailable' group and at follow-up they noted particularly the anxious, insecure attachment of the children – which was even more marked than in children who had been physically abused.

CONCLUSION

Clearly there *are* adverse consequences to teenage pregnancy. At the same time it is evident that the *major* sources of disadvantage

Table 2.7. Factors associated with 'depression or nerves' in the year following birth of their baby by teenage mothers.

	Percentage who suffered from depression or nerves between interviews	Number of women (= 100%)
Classified as:		
middle class	30	79
working class	47	315
Had a GCE:		
yes	34	91
no	45	365
Marital status:		
single	45	128
married	41	312
separated	(75)	16
Ethnic background:		
white Caucasian	45	413
Asian	23	22
West Indian	(37)	19
Had an abortion before conceiving their 'survey' baby:		
yes	67	21
no	42	434
Used birth control around the time their 'survey' baby was conceived:		
yes	58	90
no	40	364
Initial reactions to their 'survey' pregnancy:		
pleased	38	226
mixed feelings or upset	48	227
Went short of things they needed:		
yes	58	106
no	38	349
Housing considered to be:		
very suitable	35	152
fairly suitable	42	165
rather unsuitable	51	132
Number of times went out on average per week:		
never	56	55
sometimes but less than once	49	127
once	40	143
twice or more often	35	131
Marriage rated as:		
very happy	31	173
quite happy	44	105
not happy	75	28
'Survey' baby described as:		
very or fairly easy to look after	41	403
rather difficult to look after	58	40
Total sample	43	456

are not maternal age but the social circumstances of young mothers. Those adverse factors (relatively minor) which are age-specific are not more so than in significantly older mothers. In both cases the women need to be encouraged to consider their age-suitability for pregnancy. But it is not a sufficient basis for denying them the right to become mothers.

If teenage mothers are allowed to be relatively poor and unsupported then, like mothers of any age in comparable circumstances, they and their children will suffer the consequences.

3
TEENAGE
SEXUAL BEHAVIOUR

THE OPPOSITION TO RESEARCH

For a society where pornography, of various levels, flourishes and popular newspapers reflect an almost obsessional interest in the more sordid aspects of sex, we have until recently known very little about the representative reality of people's sexual behaviour in the UK.

This situation was changed by the publication in 1994 of the *first* large-scale survey in this country (Johnson *et al.*, 1994). Based on an analysis of questionnaires and interviews administered to over 18,000 people in a random sample in the UK, it provides much new information and dispels several myths (like the supposed sexual revolution of the 1960s). When there is a virtual research vacuum, prejudice, media constructions, and even public policy have to be determined by unrepresentative fragments of information.

Not the least remarkable thing about the study by Johnson and her colleagues was the level of opposition to the research being carried out at all. Government intervention stopped the relevant research council from making the necessary award (survey research is expensive) and the researchers were told that 'in all the circumstances it is not appropriate for the Government to support it and, more generally, that it would not be right for the Government to support the survey' (*ibid.*, p. 16). This extraordinary turn of events was capped by the rapid decision of the Wellcome Foundation to support the research to the tune of £900,000. Much credit is due to the Foundation for that action.

The most remarkable aspect of the episode was that all this took place at a time when there was mounting concern about the scale of teenage pregnancy and the spread of HIV infection, both of which the Government was committed to tackle as social/medical problems.

27

An effective policy approach to both problems requires an accurate and representative picture of present-day sexual behaviour in the UK. *Unless you know the circumstances and practices of human sexuality you cannot mitigate undesirable consequences.* In particular you cannot target 'at risk' populations – surely essential for cost-effective intervention.

The opposition to human sexuality research is widespread and remarkable in its irrationality.

The first large-scale surveys were carried out by Dr Alfred Kinsey and his colleagues in the US after the last war (Kinsey and Pomeroy *et al.*, 1948, 1953). Their publication provoked a scandalized (and fascinated) response. By the standards of modern survey research they were poorly carried out (Kinsey took his subjects where he could find them) but at least his data were *empirical*. Perhaps the main effect of this early research was to demonstrate the great *range* and diversity of character of human sexual expression. The accepted 'norms' clearly didn't apply to reality. It was in the 1950s, not the 1960s, that sexual behaviour responded to these major shifts in cultural awareness, and this may provide the background to what disturbs people: the tension that exists between the 'real' and the 'ideal'.

Denial is a very basic defence in human psychology: people deny admitting things about themselves, about others and about society at large. In a sense many people may not *want* to know the truth about human sexual behaviour. There is a real ambivalence here because, paradoxically, there is a ready market for dubious journalistic 'surveys' of the more extravagant aspects of sexual behaviour presumably designed to titillate the appetites of the readership. The US Committee on AIDS research (cited by Johnson *et al.*, pp. 3–4) comments that: 'Research quackery abounds . . . such "reports" are transient sources of fun, fantasy and profit – a short flash in the media pan.'

Perhaps the reason for this apparent ambivalence is that no one takes these 'fun' surveys seriously, whereas 'serious' surveys can have a special kind of power. Johnson *et al.* (*ibid.*, p. 12) put this rather well:

> Some of the political disquiet about surveys of sexual
> behaviour may be associated with the power of survey
> information to change moral norms, and the difficulty
> of maintaining ethical values in the face of evidence

that considerable proportions of the populace feel or behave differently.

SEX AND SOCIETY

The drive to sexual activity is biologically determined but it is a mistake to think simply or even mainly in biological terms. The enormous variation in sexual behaviour within our society, between different societies or groups, and across time can only be explained in terms of learning – of cultural and sub-cultural influence.

It is true that young people are reaching sexual maturity earlier. The age of menarche is now typically around the age of 12, whereas at the beginning of this century it was around 14 (Tanner, 1962) but that is not sufficient to account for the present level of teenage conceptions.

Indeed, the seeds of hope are here. If sexual behaviour was something biologically 'fixed' then there would be little we could do about it. However, potentially, what is learned can be learned differently, even though the changing of learned behaviour is no easy matter – particularly where it is pleasurable.

ADOLESCENT SEXUAL BEHAVIOUR

Most of the data in what follows are drawn from Johnson *et al.*, 1994. To prevent tedious repetition this is not further acknowledged except where sense requires it. Where other sources are used these are referenced as such.

Because pregnancy depends on sexual intercourse it is easy to focus on first intercourse as the beginning of sexual activity. But those things – like kissing, cuddling and touching – which in adults are usually the preliminaries to sexual intercourse are, for young adolescents, often an end in themselves.

In the interview section of their study Johnson and her colleagues asked two questions of relevance here:

- 'How old were you when you first had sexual intercourse with someone of the opposite sex or hasn't this happened?'
- 'How old were you when you first had any type of experience of a sexual kind – for example, kissing, cuddling, petting – with someone of the opposite sex (or hasn't this happened either)?'

In addition those interviewed were asked about:

• the age of their partner at that first time;
• whether it was the first time for them;
• whether contraception was used.

The research focused on sexual intercourse that occurred *after* the age of 13 but it is worth noting here that 1.2 per cent of men and 0.4 per cent of women reported experiencing sexual intercourse *before* the age of 13.

AGE AT FIRST INTERCOURSE

Despite the undoubted relaxation of sexual taboos, the first experience of intercourse is still accorded great personal and social significance. Much research testifies to the very clear memories of the first experience that people retain throughout their lives. It is likely therefore that the *accuracy* of such data is good.

Earlier research in the UK (e.g. Schofield, 1965; Farrell, 1978; Dunnell, 1979) provided evidence of major changes in age at first intercourse during the past 40 or 50 years. Three trends were apparent:

• a progressive reduction in age at first intercourse;
• an increase in the number of young women having their first experiences *before* the age of legal consent;
• an 'equalizing' in the behaviour of men and women – men having typically been more experienced than women.

The new research confirmed this picture.

Of the *youngest* women interviewed in the sample, aged 16–19, the median age for first intercourse was 17; amongst women aged 55–59 (born 1931–35) the median age was 21 – a four-year difference. A similar comparison for men showed a three-year drop comparing the same age groups.

A different kind of comparison is possible by taking the data from the earlier studies by Schofield, and Farrell (*op. cit.*).

Table 3.1. Percentage of young people in the age range 15–19 reporting sexual intercourse by age 16.

Author and date* of survey	Men	Women
Schofield 1964	14%	5%
Farrell 1974	31%	12%
Johnson 1990	27.6%	18.7%

* = date of *survey*, not date of publication.

Farrell reported a possible tendency for boys to exaggerate in his study. Be that as it may, the most striking change is in the sexual experiences of young women: and it is women who get pregnant. Table 3.2 (also from Johnson *et al.*, p. 74) gives the full data for first sexual intercourse before the age of 16 for the different age ranges interviewed: the progressive character of the data needs no further comment.

Table 3.2. First sexual intercourse before the age of 16 by current age

Age at interview	Women		Men	
	(%)	Base	(%)	Base
16–19	18.7	971	27.6	827
20–24	14.7	1251	23.8	1137
25–29	10.0	1519	23.8	1126
30–34	8.6	1349	23.2	1012
35–39	5.8	1261	18.4	982
40–44	4.3	1277	14.5	1042
45–49	3.4	1071	13.9	827
50–54	1.4	933	8.9	684
55–59	0.8	716	5.8	603

The 'current' picture is demonstrated in Figure 3.1 (also from Johnson *et al.*, p. 74) which shows age at first intercourse for men and women who were in the age range 16–24 at time of interview. Note the considerable variation, including the approximately 20 per cent of both sexes who had not yet experienced heterosexual intercourse – evidence of the cultural diversity of sexual experience.

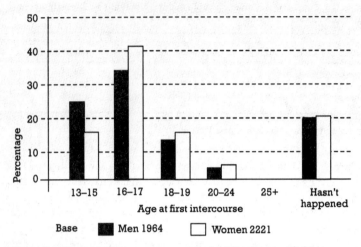

Figure 3.1. Age at first intercourse: respondents' age range 16–24

WHY HAS AGE AT FIRST INTERCOURSE DECLINED?

The answers to this may seem so obvious that it is hardly worth asking the question in the first place. But the 'obvious' sometimes just isn't correct, as is the case here.

Much is made of the formal and informal 'liberalization' of sexual behaviour in the 1960s. During that decade there were important changes in statute relating, for example, to homosexuality and abortion, relaxations of censorship and the like. The advent of improved methods of contraception, particularly 'the pill' also occurred at this time. Johnson *et al.* (*op. cit.*, p. 79) point out that the steepest decline in age at first intercourse for women – by two years – occurred during the 1950s. Indeed it fell as much during that decade as over the next 30 years; this is also true for men.

It has also been assumed that, in particular, the advent of oral contraception was a causal factor in increased sexual activity and a reduction in the age of onset of sexual activity. But although the pill was available from 1961 for married women, in practice it was not available for unmarried women until 1972. This is well past the point when sexual norms had undergone their major revolution. In any case, a large number of empirical studies (cited by Johnson *et al.*, p. 79) found no association between pill use and level of sexual activity.

The assumption that the availability of contraception and abortion services have a direct 'causal' effect on sexual activity is not borne out by the empirical evidence. More than that, it presumes a more rational basis for 'decisions' to have sexual intercourse than is in fact the case (see Chapter 4).

SOCIAL CLASS

As we saw in Chapter 1, teenagers from the 'manual' social classes are much more likely to become pregnant as young teenagers, and are also more likely to carry the baby to term.

Age at first intercourse has declined for both sexes and all classes over the past 40 years but a marked social class difference remains, as can be seen from Table 3.3 which gives the median age at first intercourse by social class for the age group 16–24.

Table 3.3. Median age at first intercourse by social class for the age group 16–24. (Johnson *et al.*, p. 81.)

Social class	I	II	III NM	III M	IV	V	Other	Base
Men	18	17	17	16	16	16	18	1472
Women	18	17	17	17	16	16	17	1863

The implication of this is simple: *young women in the 'manual' social classes are much more at risk of becoming teenage mothers than their middle-class counterparts*, even allowing for social class differences in the use of contraceptive and abortion services: both of which are more likely to be used by middle-class teenagers (see Chapter 5).

What the more recent data also reflect is the 'equalization' process of the two sexes referred to elsewhere; and *which works particularly to the disadvantage of women in Social Classes IV and V*.

In the oldest age group (45–59) interviewed in the Johnson *et al.* study there was a difference of *three* years between the two sexes for age of first intercourse in Social Class V and *two* years in Social Class IV. In the 16–24 age group this difference had entirely disappeared.

EDUCATIONAL LEVEL

Social class and educational level are highly correlated – much more so than we would like to think in our egalitarian society. But they are not the same and a number of researchers (e.g. Wilson, Brown and Richards, 1992) have commented on the need to raise the educational prospects of working-class girls so that they can have good reasons for deferring sexual activity and pregnancy. This equation may, of course, be too simple as sexual behaviour seems to be determined by multiple sub-cultural factors.

The evidence from the Johnson study (pp. 82–83) is that the 'effects' of educational attainment are there but are less marked than social class differences. Table 3.4 gives the median age at first intercourse by educational level for the 16–24 age group.

Table 3.4. Median age at first intercourse by educational level for the age range 16–24

Education	Degree	A-level	O-level/CSE	Other	None	Base
Men	18	17	16	17	16	1471
Women	18	17	17	17	16	1862

ETHNIC AND RELIGIOUS GROUP MEMBERSHIP

Ethnic differences in age at first intercourse are more marked than the effects of religious group membership, particularly for women.

Table 3.5 below is constructed from data in the Johnson *et al.* study (p. 84).

Table 3.5. Proportion of respondents reporting first sexual intercourse before 16 by ethnic group and religion (all age groups)

Ethnic group	Men %	Women %
White	18.9	8.0
Black	26.3	9.6
Pakistani Bangladeshi Indian	10.7	1.1
Religion		
All religious groups	18.8	7.8
No affiliation	22.7	12.3

Religious and ethnic groupings are inter-related, as are to some extent social class and educational level, but there is also a cumulative effect, e.g. educational level plus religious group membership. The significance of ethnic group is particularly noticeable in the case of people originating from the Indian sub-continent.

THE EXPERIENCE OF FIRST INTERCOURSE

The issue of contraceptive use by teenagers is discussed in full in Chapter 5 but it is relevant here as part of the experience of first intercourse. In the Johnson *et al.* study approximately 20 per cent of the young women reported *not* using contraception on their first experience – this is a lower rate than the similar reports from older age groups. Young women of today are more contraception conscious. A similar trend is apparent for men although, as might be expected, they are marginally less likely to have used contraception with their first partner.

The situation for *under*-16s, however, is a different matter and at this age level Johnson *et al.* point out that where this is the case 'nearly half of young women and more than half of young men report no method used either by themselves or their partner . . . It emphasizes the particular vulnerability of this group to unplanned pregnancy' (p. 87).

They report that the failure to use contraception at first intercourse was *less* common for those with a regular partner. The converse is a situation of sexual exploitation of young women.

AGE OF PARTNER AT FIRST INTERCOURSE

The pattern is different for men as opposed to women. Johnson *et al.* report that:

- 'Men's partners at first intercourse tend to be roughly the same age as themselves', i.e., the general picture.
- However, 'The older the man was at first intercourse the more likely it was to have taken place with a partner younger than himself . . .'
- 'there is no evidence of widespread initiation of young men into sex by older women.'
- 'For women . . . an older partner at first intercourse is the norm. Of women aged 13–17 at first intercourse, 75 per cent had

partners older than themselves . . .' (*ibid.*, p. 91). Note that this does *not* contradict the first point above.

For around half of all women and around 40 per cent of men the event took place in the context of an established relationship. Fewer than 1 per cent of men and women were married at the time. *Pre-marital sex is practically universal.*

THE ISSUE OF EXPLOITATION

Because the tendency is that the younger the woman at first intercourse the older her partner will be, the issue of exploitation arises. For example, Ingham, Woodcock and Stenner (1991) in a small-scale intensive study (n = 95) of young people's experience of first intercourse and knowledge of partners report that:

> The tendency with the female respondents to have
> older partners was particularly pronounced the earlier
> in the relationship that intercourse took place. Almost
> half of the females who had intercourse within the first
> twenty-four hours (of meeting) had partners at least ten
> years older than themselves. (p. 125)

Johnson *et al.* add another dimension to that when they report that:

> More than two-thirds of women whose partner at first
> intercourse was someone they had met for the first time
> used no contraception, neither did nearly half of those
> for whom it was someone they had met recently . . . The
> increased likelihood of lack of contraception with a
> non-steady partner may be a cause for concern, as this
> is the group most likely to suffer, and least likely to wel-
> come, an unplanned pregnancy. (p. 99)

'UNPLANNED' SEXUAL ACTIVITY

At all ages the 'planning' of sexual activity is seen as more or less distasteful and as something that detracts from the emotional quality of the experience. But 'unplanned' doesn't have to mean 'unprepared'. Sex education is often not sufficiently practical, certainly at a level of detail. Least of all does it prepare young women for what they can do when they have sexual intercourse without contraception or *when contraception may have failed*.

The high rate of contraceptive failure (at all ages) is discussed in Chapter 5, as also is widespread ignorance of the use of *emergency* contraception, even in the case of experienced women. Since it is the young who are most likely to be unprepared, *knowledge of, and access to, emergency contraception is a high priority.*

THE ROMANTIC VIEW OF SEX

Sexual disappointment is one of the hidden problems in our society. Whilst a vague romanticism is no preparation for a fulfilling sexual experience, the experience of early sexual activity often appears to militate against later sexual adjustment. Almost 60 per cent of the women in the Johnson *et al.* study who had first intercourse before the age of 16 regretted it and felt it was 'too soon'. The 'exploitation' issue is relevant here. There is also evidence that early sexual intercourse is associated with cervical cancer later in life (Wynder, 1969). For these reasons an emphasis in sex education on deferring a start to sexual relationships would be of value on psychological and physical health grounds for women. And it is here that there is some evidence that sex education can be effective. As is discussed in Chapter 4, sex education appears to be ineffective in changing sexual behaviour once a pattern is established, *except in relation to contraceptive practice*. We consider that area next.

4
SEX EDUCATION

THE BACKGROUND

One of the ironies of the situation is that it has taken the AIDS epidemic, rather than the social and personal problems of teenage pregnancies, to encourage research into sexual behaviour and the means of influencing it. And even here, as we noted in Chapter 3, this has not been without conflict and controversy. Controversy and sex education go hand in hand: it is a sure topic for media interest, especially if some unfortunate professional has ventured to be a little explicit about sexual behaviour.

In the UK as in the US there is a remarkable ambivalence towards the content and emphasis in sex education and it is rare for it to be linked, even tenuously, to medical and contraceptive services. Adult attitudes typically polarize along the dimension which, at one end, fears that it will encourage promiscuity or premature sexual activity and, at the other, that without it teenagers will not be able to make informed choices. As we shall see below, both groups are mistaken in their expectations.

WHY SEX EDUCATION?

Sexual behaviour can lead to large-scale social problems, of which unintended pregnancy is just one. 'Managing' this biological drive is, and has been, a major preoccupation for all societies in recorded history. Comprehensive psychological theories have been built round it, different forms of religion have been largely defined by their stance in relation to sexuality. The present-day faith in 'education' is just one expression of the need for social control: we tend to look to the educational process to deal with some aspects of human sexuality. How successful it is in doing so, is another matter.

There is a widespread demand for information on all aspects of sexuality. The Family Planning Association receives over 200,000 enquiries annually; the 'agony aunt' in a teenage magazine claimed to receive over 1,000 letters a week on related topics from girls aged 12–18 (FPA, 1995a).

School is universally favoured as the place where sex education should take place. National surveys consistently show that around 95 per cent of parents and young people want this (Allen, 1987). However, the adequacy of school sex education, and parents' reaction when it is actually offered is another matter. As far as young people are concerned *content* and *confidentiality* are crucial. A FPA survey (BMRB, 1994) found that a majority of 13–15 year olds said they would find it useful to be able to talk to teachers about such matters as contraception, but less than a third (31 per cent) would do so if their parents were informed. And this is exactly what schools do not find themselves able to do.

The political ambivalence is apparent from the various relevant Education Acts: these are discussed more fully below. But the most recent (1993) Act gives parents the right to withdraw their child from all or any aspects of school sex education. Most young people do not agree with this (BMRB, 1994) and in research carried out for the Health Education Authority (NFER, 1994) 70 per cent of parents said they would not consider withdrawing their child. But note the gap between this percentage and those who think that schools should provide sex education.

IS SCHOOL THE MAIN SOURCE OF INFORMATION?

Any discussion of sex education has to recognize that formal education in schools can only be *one* source of information. And, as we shall see, because of the constraints on schools, young people are *obliged* to go elsewhere to seek the information that is most important to them.

Girls in particular, and the youngest teenagers in general, see their parents as an important source of information. A survey by Balding (1994) of nearly 30,000 young people aged 11–16 found that a third of the boys and almost half of the girls aged 11–12 gave their parents as their *main* source of information. But by age 15–16 this had dropped to 15 per cent for boys and 22.4 per cent for girls: and this is the age where young people are most at risk of sexual exploitation and unintended pregnancy. Overall, half the teenagers felt their parents *should* be the main source of information, but cited mutual embarrassment as the barrier.

The study by Allen (1987) found that although teenagers recognize that their friends are not a reliable source of information, it is usually where they turn first. Embarrassment is the main barrier to approaching teachers or doctors, especially if they are under age and contraception is the topic on which they seek information (because of fear of disclosure to their parents). Trust and confidentiality, as well as embarrassment, are the obstacles here: quality of advice suffers in consequence.

Magazines, particularly teenage and women's magazines in general, were found in Balding's survey (*ibid.*) to be an important source of information, particularly for girls. This is recognized, for example, by the Brook Advisory Centres which regularly advertise their helpline numbers in magazines such as *17*.

SEX EDUCATION IN SCHOOLS

Under current legislation (e.g. the Education Reform Act, 1988) sex education is *required* in secondary schools but not primary schools – although the latter are required to *consider* whether to offer sex education. At the same time sex education as such, is not part of the National Curriculum. From September 1994 the Science curriculum only includes the biology of human behaviour. *Apart from this the Secretary of State has no statutory power to prescribe the content or organization of sex education.*

Other advice is framed in very general and highly moral terms, particularly emphasizing 'family values'. For example the Education (No. 2) Act 1986 requires the Local Education Authority, the school governing body, and the head teacher, to ensure that sex education 'is given in such a manner as to encourage those pupils to have due regard to moral conditions and the value of family life' (cited in FPA, 1995b). This same Act gives school governors the responsibility for decisions on sex education in schools.

It follows from this that there is enormous scope for local prejudice to determine the content of what young people receive. Information on sexual behaviour and contraceptive practice are those areas most constrained; and this is reflected in the opinions of young people. In a survey of over 7,000 16–19 year olds a high proportion (38–46 per cent) felt that their schools had not provided enough information on homosexuality, AIDS, abortion, and sexuality (Rudat, 1992).

Advice on contraception, particularly at an individual level, is the most restricted. *Circular 5/94* (DFE, 1994) which interprets the 1993 Education Act for education authorities states, in relation to contraceptive advice to under-age pupils, that: 'The general rule must be that giving an individual pupil advice on such matters without parental knowledge or consent would be an inappropriate exercise of a teacher's professional responsibilities' (p. 14, para. 39).

The same document also specified that such pupil confidences should be relayed to the head teacher and parents (para. 40) even though there was no tested legal basis for this. Legal advice on this point sought by teachers' unions concluded, however, that teachers were not bound by this *unless* they were under a contractual obligation to do so (Sex Education Forum, 1994). A distinction was also drawn in law between *giving* advice and giving information on *sources* of advice – which could be done whether or not parents had withdrawn their children from sex education classes.

The certainty and confidence of teachers in *their* rights and their ability to deal with problems of sexuality at an educational level are central to the quality and character of sex education.

This is not the place to review the range of sex education programmes on offer: details are given in Appendix A. However, the manual: *Developing Sex Education in Schools: A Practical Guide* (Mullinar, 1994) published by the Family Planning Association, is just one recent example of the high quality programmes available. The question, however, is: what do such programmes achieve?

EDUCATION AND SEXUAL BEHAVIOUR

A review by Kirby (1989) of *evaluated* sex education programmes concluded that:

> The findings are nearly unanimous – instruction in sex education does increase factual knowledge about sexuality . . . Although many different teaching approaches were evaluated in these studies, there was no convincing evidence that one approach was more effective at increasing knowledge than other approaches. (p. 165)

Although such programmes do increase knowledge it is a common finding that adolescents knew quite a lot before the programme started. So the notion that they exist in a state of vulnerable ignorance is probably mistaken (*op. cit.,* p. 165).

The real question at issue is the relationship between sex education and sexual behaviour, particularly in relation to pregnancy risk. Miller (1995) in a recent review concludes: 'virtually no evidence supports the idea that sex education will result in a change in adolescent sexual behaviour' (pp. 1525–6).

A review of sex education carried out at John Hopkins University (Dawson, 1986) concludes specifically that: 'neither pregnancy education nor contraception education exerts any significant effect on the risk of premarital pregnancy among sexually active teenagers' (p. 168).

Perhaps we should conclude that education *alone* does not seem to reduce the risk of adolescent pregnancy which, as we saw in Chapter 2, appears to be determined by a multiplicity of factors including a range of pressures within the teenager's social environment.

CHANGING KNOWLEDGE AND CHANGING BEHAVIOUR

Schools and universities are, on the whole, excellent places for acquiring knowledge – although some are much better than others. But even sophisticated adults find it difficult to take the knowledge learnt in this abstract fashion and interpret it and relate it to the detail of their social lives. This 'abstractness' is one element in the difficulty. The other, and more important, is the less-than-straightforward relationship between knowledge and behaviour. This has been discussed by the author elsewhere (Gillham and Thomson, 1996) in the context of child safety and what is usually called 'medical compliance'. Health education assumes this 'knowledge enhancement' perspective: implicit in this is that, given knowledge, people will change their unsafe, unhealthy, risk-taking behaviours. Educated middle-class adults are most responsive to this kind of appeal – occasionally to their disadvantage when the 'scare' emphasis is misplaced. But most people are not, unless it is reflected in a change in that elusive quality, social *fashion*.

Kirby (*op.cit.*), for example, refers to several studies which evaluated nutrition education in schools, found significant increases in knowledge, but no significant change in eating habits (p. 168). Davies and Coggans (1991) found the same problem in a large-scale secondary school-based drug education programme in Scotland.

This does not mean that we entirely discount sex education as a factor in changing sexual behaviour and preventing teenage pregnancy. It means we need to understand what kind of sex education could work in the social context which influences behaviour. Macdonald (1987) suggests that typically sex education does not reflect current knowledge about the multiple forces that influence teenage sexual behaviour and that because it does not 'fit' it can do little to reduce premarital pregnancy.

'RATIONALITY' AND 'DECISIONS' ABOUT SEXUAL BEHAVIOUR

The entire edifice of health and personal safety education is based on the assumption that 'right' choices will follow from good quality information. The implicit notion is that decisions are made on the basis of the information available to an individual. Spelt out like that it is a notion that is manifestly untrue, at least in certain domains of behaviour. This is not to say that people are 'irrational' – whether adolescent or adult – but that we misunderstand the relation between rationality and behaviour (Ingham, 1994).

Loewenstein and Furstenberg (1991) in a paper entitled: 'Is teenage sexual behaviour rational?' present three main reasons for teenagers behaving in the way they do:

• decision-making at this age is typically reactive, impulsive and unplanned with an emphasis placed on the importance of 'spontaneity';
• 'it is possible that sexual behaviour, whether by teenagers or adults, does not lend itself to interpretation as rational choice. Like food, alcohol, drugs, and cigarettes, sex is commonly associated with impulsivity ... when people seem to display a striking indifference to their own long-term interest' (pp. 961–2);
• the *immediate* 'cost', e.g. discomfort or distaste for birth control methods, can be more potent than the (delayed) possibility of pregnancy.

This last point is a very important one, and accounts for much 'unsafe' or 'unhealthy' or otherwise 'irrational' decision-making. Whether using a seat belt, taking your medicine or giving up cigarettes, *long-term* benefits may be (and commonly are) largely disregarded in favour of relatively minor immediate 'benefits' – avoiding the constriction of a seat belt or being 'calmed' by a cigarette.

This is the 'micro' perspective. We need to stand back and take the wider 'macro' perspective.

TEENAGE PREGNANCY: THE LESSONS FROM INTERNATIONAL COMPARISONS

Although the database is now a little out of date, the international comparison study of 37 (Western) nations by Jones *et al.* (1986) remains the most important single study of teenage pregnancy. Perhaps the most dramatic finding was the enormous variation in teenage pregnancy rates between different countries. The following graph (Figure 4.1) shows the rates for the most directly comparable countries.

It can be seen that the rates for US teenagers are *twice* those for the UK which are themselves *three times* the rates for the Netherlands. Note that these are *pregnancies*, not births, and so are not modified by variations in the availability of abortion services.

More recent comparative data between the UK and the Netherlands (Forum for Family Planning 1994, cited in Jacobson, Wilkinson and Pill, 1995) show the gap to be even wider with the Netherlands rate being nine pregnancies per 1,000 women under 20 compared with *69* per 1,000 in the UK.

The differences are not to be explained by variations in the frequency of sexual intercourse amongst teenagers. The major differences (which are interlinked) are:

- the more extensive public health and welfare benefits in countries other than the US;
- the existence of a large economically deprived underclass in the US;
- greater emphasis on sex education and contraception services *particularly* in countries with the lowest rates;
- the greater openness and acceptance of teenage sexuality, again especially in those countries with the lowest rates;
- more liberal abortion policies (but not more *per capita* abortions) in the countries with the lowest rates.

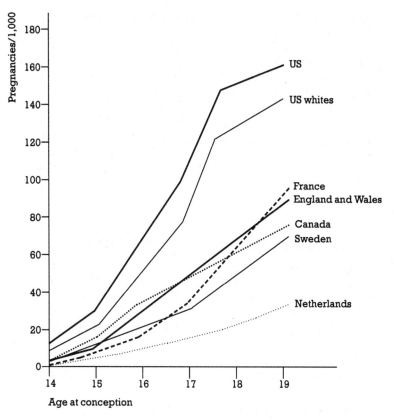

Figure 4.1. Teenage pregnancy rates per 1,000 women for selected countries 1980.

These differences reflect major political emphases: a greater emphasis on equality and broadly-based welfare provision *together with* a lack of ambivalence in the attitudes and services that teenagers encounter. It is within this broad framework that sex education has to be seen as effective or not. This does not mean that local initiatives cannot be effective (some are described and discussed below) but that national-level and nationwide shifts in attitudes, policy and provision are necessary before adolescent pregnancy prevention can become a comprehensive reality.

SPECIFIC PROGRAMME EVALUATIONS

Most thoroughgoing evaluations have been carried out in the US. Their applicability to other countries has to be qualified because levels of severe deprivation are higher in the US and rates of teenage pregnancy are also much higher. It is easier to demonstrate the effectiveness of an intervention when the position starts out as an extreme one. The better the initial pre-intervention situation, the harder it is to make further improvement. But this is more to do with how much improvement is possible than what seems to characterize an effective intervention. So, with this qualification in mind, we can consider what lessons can be learnt from the US research.

FOUR PROGRAMMES THAT WORKED

1. *The St Paul Project*. This was part of a comprehensive project (the St Paul Maternal and Infant Care Project: Edwards *et al.*, 1980) which incorporated a school-linked clinic providing a contraception service to teenagers. Beginning in 1968 the first effect was a reduction in the school dropout rate (from 43 per cent to 10 per cent over a *three-year* period). As the programme developed its impact the birth rate dropped for the junior/senior high school girls, from 59 per 1,000 in 1976 to 26 per 1,000 in 1984 (American Public Welfare Association, 1986).

2. *The Baltimore Pregnancy Prevention Programme for Urban Teenagers*. This programme, based in a junior and senior high school, was also linked to a nearby clinic. Group and individual counselling was provided and sexuality and contraceptive education was introduced in the classroom by a nurse and a social worker; advice on contraception was provided in the clinic.

   Each of the two schools was paired with an equivalent school in the city. A 30 per cent reduction in pregnancy was found in the girls who had been involved in the programme for three years; overall rates dropped in the participating schools but *increased* in the comparison schools (Hirsch *et al.*, 1987). Other 'spin-offs' were apparent, notably more teenagers finishing school.

   However, the same group of researchers (Zabin *et al.*, 1986) concluded that 'junior high may be too late to affect sexual onset for about half of those boys and girls, or indeed, to reach the sexually active among them in their high-risk early period of exposure' (p. 86). Most of the 7th/8th grade boys in the study, i.e. those aged 13–14 years, had already engaged in sex. As noted earlier, sexual behaviour is difficult to modify once established. For this reason the next study is of specific interest.

3. *Postponing Sexual Involvement.* This counselling and curriculum programme in Atlanta, Georgia was explicitly focused on supporting teenagers in postponing the initiation of sexual intercourse. Targeted on 7th/8th grade students it decreased sexual involvement in 8th grades by a factor of four to five times compared with teenagers who did not have the programme (Howard and Mitchell, 1993). However it was *not* simply an 'abstinence only' programme – a type which does not appear to work (like 'say no' programmes in other areas such as drug abuse). According to the authors the programme 'provides information designed to help adolescents explore attitudes and feelings about managing physical feelings within a relationship. It also teaches adolescents skills to resist social and peer pressures to become sexually involved' (*op. cit.,* p. 116).

The actual programme had a number of features which may have contributed to its success, notably the use of 'peer educators' from nearby high schools to teach the curriculum in the junior high schools. Overall the programme seems to have been characterized by:

- very clear objectives (not least to the student);
- an exceptional degree of sensitivity to the issues involved.

One outcome of interest which validated the objective of delaying initiation was that the programme had *no* impact on students whose sexual careers had begun before the course started.

4. *The South Carolina Programme.* This project produced some of the most dramatic results for any programme of its type. Where it differed was in the level of promotion of the main messages in the programme and its community-wide character.

In part this was made possible because a relatively small rural county was selected with only about 325 females in the 14–17 age range. The *content* of the programme was conventional enough but it involved parents, churches, schools, the media and other community organizations. This 'saturation' approach – akin to an advertising campaign – was evaluated by comparing the pregnancy rates for two years *before* the programme with those three years *after*. Pregnancy rates had dropped by half (Vincent, Clearie and Schlucter, 1987).

Note that it was the method of promotion rather than the content of the messages which seemed to have the impact – combined with an exceptionally unanimous level of co-operation amongst very different interested groups.

CONCLUSION

The last 30 years have taught us that education cannot change society. The problems created by social conditions severely restrict the impact of almost any kind of educational programme. Sex education is no exception to that. But given the limits, a number of features emerge from programmes which have had an impact.

1. The importance of linking sex education to practical advice on contraception and easily accessible contraceptive services.
2. Targeting sex education on those who have not yet begun their sexual careers – whether or not delaying onset is the aim. At this stage teenagers appear to be open to influence.
3. Using a counselling as well as a tutorial approach to the teenage clients.
4. Establishing a wide level of agreement and support in the community on the aims and nature of the programme.
5. Making the messages and objectives clear and explicit.
6. Adopting a higher profile 'advertising style' approach.

One particular message, not evaluated in these programmes, is concerned with the use, nature and availability of emergency contraception. This is discussed more fully in Chapter 5 but it is clear from recent research (Pearson *et al.*, 1995) that not only teenagers but adults are remarkably ignorant of the range of post-coital contraceptives available and the scope of their use (Whitlow, Desmond and Hay, 1995).

5

CONTRACEPTION AND ABORTION

THE CURRENT REALITY

> What if it were arranged that adolescent girls, from
> puberty . . . could not become pregnant unless they
> made a deliberate conscious choice to do so? . . . This
> is conjecture only in one sense: we are probably politi-
> cally incapable of making it happen . . . we already
> have the technology available now that would make this
> possible. This technology . . . involves long-term con-
> traception which is 'automatic' in its function: it works
> at the time regardless of what the user does . . . It is this
> feature of user independence that makes true long-
> term contraception ideal for young or inexperienced
> users. (Battin, 1995, p. 1204)

This quotation from a recent editorial in the US journal *Social
Science and Medicine* serves as a reference point for the current
reality of pregnancy prevention (and not just for teenagers).

The 'automatic' devices that Battin refers to are 'Norplant' – a
long-acting progestogen implanted as capsules under the skin in
the arm, slowly releasing a low dose of the hormone and effective
for five years; and the intra-uterine device (IUD) – specifically the
Copper T380, which is effective for up to eight years. Both devices
are normally easily removed and therefore, reversible. 'Norplant'
has been available in the UK since late in 1993. The IUDs in current
use originated in the 1980s but have been progressively refined
since then.

Even allowing for the utopian flavour of the editorial quoted
above, the gap between what is technically possible and what happens in practice is remarkable. The 1995–96 Annual Report of the

Brook Advisory Centres (a charity established specifically to offer a contraceptive service to those under 25) reported that of 76,759 clients in 1995–96 just 695 were fitted with an IUD; and an unspecified proportion of 1,723 were fitted with 'Norplant' (probably less than a quarter).

Since those young people who attend a Brook Centre are a self-selected minority of all teenagers, certainly not typical, the representative situation is probably even more dramatically different.

ABORTION AND CONTRACEPTIVE FAILURE

The gap between the technologically possible and the actual situation is reflected in abortion statistics. Table 1.2 (p. 5) gives numbers and rates for termination of pregnancy in married and unmarried women in England and Wales for 1994.

Clearly the biological drive towards reproduction is not easily defeated, even when it is unwanted. An abortion rate of around 25 per cent overall has to be a minimum estimate of unwanted pregnancies. Many more women, for one reason or another, good or bad, will have gone to term. An unwanted pregnancy does not, of course, mean an unwanted baby. Babies, fortunately for them, have the knack of justifying their existence when they arrive. As we saw in Chapter 2, most of the teenage mothers in the Simms and Smith study (*ibid.*) professed themselves delighted with their babies, even though more than a half of them (54 per cent) described their pregnancy as 'unwanted' – 73 per cent in the case of those who were still unmarried at the time their baby was born.

Even if abortion avoids the long-term costs of babies who were unwanted, the immediate economic cost of around 170,000 abortions a year (Government Statistical Service, 1996) to the NHS has to be judged as money that could have been better spent on contraceptive services. However, the provision of contraceptive services, particularly to the young and unmarried, is a matter for even more political and ethical ambivalence than sex education, were that possible. As in other areas, in order to understand the present we have to delve into the past.

A GLIMPSE AT HISTORY

The present-day difficulties that surround the provision of an adequate pregnancy prevention service for teenagers – which are linked to the inadequacies of sex education (see Chapter 4) – can only be understood by looking at the recent history of contraceptive service provision. The picture is one of extreme moral and political confusion, and a level of provision which has always lagged far behind what would appear to be required by changes in sexual behaviour, levels of fertility, and the social and personal problems of unintended pregnancies.

The first birth control clinic in the UK was established by Dr Marie Stopes in London in 1921, amidst controversy that ensured her name remains well known even today. The National Birth Control Council, the immediate predecessor of the present-day Family Planning Association, was established in 1930. By its very title the character of the FPA was identified as a means of spacing and controlling pregnancies for married women; and this view was predominant in the FPA for more than a generation. At the time of writing in 1997 the organization's title remains the same, even if the actual character of the organization has been revolutionized.

It was not until 1967, in the face of large increases in pregnancies to unmarried women (and particularly teenagers), that the government gave local health authorities the formal power to provide a contraceptive service to unmarried women on social rather than strictly medical grounds. The FPA did not reverse its own policy against providing a service to unmarried women until 1968; and it did not require its clinics actually to provide such a service until 1970 (Jones *et al.*, 1986). It is a good example of how an organization, revolutionary in its time, became a conservative force in its maturity.

Because the FPA would not provide a service to young, unmarried people, the Brook Advisory Centres were set up in 1964 and have remained at the forefront of clinic provision and education for this age group, although their clinics are far from providing a comprehensive service for young people outside the main centres of population.

The Brook 'style' inevitably influenced the FPA which is now essentially an information and education service (including a wide range of materials for young people) – a role which it fulfils very well. However, the Brook Centres, almost certainly because they have the validating experience of daily clinic provision and face-to-face encounters with young clients, seem to have a knack for identifying such key issues as ignorance of emergency contraception and the 'confidentiality' problem for young people discussed in Chapters 4 and 6.

It was not until 1974 that the NHS in the UK made contraceptive advice and supplies available to all, free of charge – again in the face of the enormous economic and social costs of unintended pregnancies. And in the late 1990s we are still far from providing an effective service, in particular for the young. For example, in 1996 there were still only 18 Brook Advisory Centres in the UK (including one in Jersey, recently established in the face of some local opposition). In the financial year 1995–96 a total of 76,759 clients were seen: only a fraction of those young people who could benefit from such a service. However, before we go on to consider the level of service need, we have to look at existing contraceptive use by teenagers.

CONTRACEPTIVE USE BY TEENAGERS

The most important source of data is the 1994 study by Johnson *et al.*, previously cited.

The notion that teenagers are ignorant of birth control methods and generally fail to use contraception is mistaken. The study cited reports that:

> More than nine out of 10 sexually active 16- to 24-year-old men and women reported the use of at least one method in the past year, compared with two-thirds of men and just over half of women in the oldest age group (many of whom will no longer be of child-bearing age) ... Compared with those who were married, contraceptive use was higher among the single or cohabiting, lower among those who were divorced or separated and lowest among the widowed, reflecting varying levels of sexual activity and need for protection against pregnancy in these groups ... (p. 297)

Methods used by those under 25 are shown in Table 5.1 (data from Johnson *et al.*, p. 298).

Table 5.1. Contraceptive methods used in the last year by 16–24 year olds, separately for men and women

Method	Men (%)	Women (%)
Pill	53.1	64.1
IUD	2.2	3.1
Condom	60.8	41.9
Diaphragm	1.8	1.0
Pessaries	0.3	0.5
Sponge	0.3	0.1
Douche	0.5	0.2
Safe period	3.9	2.3
Withdrawal	9.4	6.6
Female sterilizaton	0.5	0.4
Vasectomy	0.1	1.1
Abstinence	2.6	1.7
Other method	0.4	0.9
None	9.0	9.5
Base	1439	1692

The age range 16–24 does, of course, comprise a heterogeneous group, and within this group contraceptive practice varies with age. In the Johnson study data were collected on the use of contraception at first heterosexual intercourse. They found that where intercourse had occurred before the age of 16 nearly half of the young women and more than half of the young men reported no method used either by themselves or their partner. Over the age of 16 this proportion fell to 32 per cent for women and 36 per cent for men.

Because the experience of first intercourse is usually a well-remembered event, such data are likely to be valid. In the case of under-16s it emphasizes the particular vulnerability of this group to pregnancy. This vulnerability is enhanced by the severe limitations of sex education and counselling in schools discussed in Chapter 4.

Zabin, Kantner and Zelnik (1979) in a US study pointed out that half of all premarital pregnancies occurred in the first six months of sexual activity – indicating the importance of early contraceptive education and provision. There is no comparable UK research on this point and the data are not recent, but are consistent with related findings in the Johnson study.

CONTRACEPTIVE USE BY MARITAL STATUS

Patterns of contraceptive use vary with age, the main break in the pattern occurring in the mid-30s: it is here that male and female sterilization becomes much more common. Not surprisingly these methods are rarely involved in the under-25 age group.

However, the sharpest contrast in method of use is by marital status rather than age. Again we abstract data from the study by Johnson and her associates (1994, p. 299). Table 5.2 shows contraceptive method used in the past year by marital status.

Table 5.2. Contraceptive methods used in the last year by marital status, separately for men and women

	Married (%)	Cohabit. opp. sex (%)	Widowed (%)	Divorced, separated (%)	Single (%)	All (%)
Men						
Pill	21.3	51.9	15.7	26.7	48.7	30.4
IUD	5.6	5.7	5.0	5.9	2.5	4.9
Condom	27.9	31.0	32.4	37.1	64.2	36.9
Diaphragm	1.8	2.9	0.0	1.6	2.1	2.0
Pessaries	0.7	1.3	0.0	0.2	0.3	0.6
Sponge	0.0	0.2	0.0	0.2	0.3	0.1
Douche	0.0	0.5	0.0	1.3	0.3	0.2
Safe period	2.1	3.8	7.7	3.2	3.9	2.7
Withdrawal	5.4	10.0	7.3	8.5	9.3	6.8
Female sterilization	11.9	7.8	0.0	12.6	1.1	9.1
Vasectomy	18.2	7.5	6.8	9.2	0.1	12.8
Abstinence	1.0	2.5	0.0	1.7	2.4	1.5
Other method	0.2	1.3	0.0	0.6	0.4	0.3

In this table, as in the previous one, percentages sum to more than 100 per cent because some respondents reported more than one method. However, it is clear that *in the main* people tend to rely on one particular method.

In the case of the young and the single the use of the IUD (particularly reliable and 'behaviour-free') is very low. 'Norplant' does not figure because its use was not licensed in the UK at the time of the survey. Note also that *withdrawal* (the least reliable method) is most common amongst those who are single or co-habiting.

The analysis of the reports in the study showed that three methods predominated:

- the pill (28.8 per cent of women; 30.4 per cent of men);
- the condom (25.9 per cent of women; 36.9 per cent of men);
- sterilization (23.3 per cent of women; 21.4 per cent of men).

Johnson *et al.* report that no other single method is reported by more than 10 per cent of respondents.

The marked increase in the use of condoms, particularly amongst the young, is probably due to a number of factors:

- the wide publicity about their use as a protection against sexually transmitted diseases;
- their ready availability without prescription and without embarrassment (and there is a lesson to be learnt here);
- relative ignorance and uncertainty about other methods (some of which are more effective for contraceptive purposes).

CONTRACEPTIVE USE AND TEENAGE SEXUAL BEHAVIOUR

A general finding is that contraception is used most consistently and reliably when there is a 'steady' relationship, where sexual intercourse is an expected and predictable part of the relationship. But teenage sexual behaviour (particularly amongst the younger teenagers) is often sporadic and unplanned. This militates against regular, effective use, and also use of the more effective methods.

Pearson *et al.* (1995) in a study of 147 teenagers with unplanned pregnancies found that 80 per cent claimed to have been using contraception at the time of conception. This user percentage is close to the general data on contraceptive use by teenagers reported in the Johnson study. At the very least it indicates that contraceptive use does not mean effective contraceptive practice. The authors argue that teenagers should be encouraged to use postcoital emergency contraception where there is any possibility of contraceptive failure.

Whitlow, Desmond and Hay (1995) interviewed 100 each of men and women patients at St George's Hospital, London. Of the women (age range 15–48) 85 had heard of emergency contraception but 11 of those had the misconception that the so-called 'morning after' pill was effective only up to 12 hours after intercourse, when in fact its period of effective use is 72 hours. And only *five* of the women were aware that the intra-uterine device (IUD) could be used very effectively as a form of emergency contraception up to five days after intercourse.

Emergency contraception is of particular relevance to those whose birth control methods are not well established. The recent annual reports of the Family Planning Association (FPA, 1996) and the Brook Advisory Centres (1996a) highlight the widespread ignorance of these methods which were the subject of a recent national advertising campaign.

The Brook Annual Report 1996 commented on the continued upward trend in requests for emergency contraception:

> Although Brook encourages young people to seek con-
> traceptive advice before they become sexually active,
> and to always use condoms, the reality remains that
> first intercourse is often unplanned and unprotected.
> EC therefore plays an important role in helping to mini-
> mize the risk of unwanted pregnancy while bringing
> young people into contact with a service where they
> can sort out their on-going contraceptive needs. Inter-
> estingly, the campaign research found that 63% of
> 16–24 year olds thought schools were the ideal source
> of information about EC, but a Brook survey of clients in
> 1995 revealed that two-thirds had received no informa-
> tion about EC at school. (p. 9)

TEENAGE RELUCTANCE TO USE CONTRACEPTIVE SERVICES

If potential clients are reluctant to use a service, that has to say something about the nature of the service itself. As we saw earlier there has been outright opposition or, at least, unwillingness to provide a contraceptive service to the unmarried and, especially, the young. This conservative opposition has lost ground but is still powerful. In 1981 in the US, for example, on a rising tide of conservative resentment about the increasing number of teenage pregnancies, Richard Schweiker, President Reagan's newly appointed Secretary of Health and Human Services, declared that doctors treating unmarried teenagers under Medicaid should not be permitted to prescribe contraceptives (Gress-Wright, 1993). This was rapidly retracted but it is significant that the statement was made at all.

At around the same time in the UK and on a different level, a Mrs Victoria Gillick (possessed of five daughters under the age of 16) brought a much-publicized court case seeking to prohibit doctors from prescribing contraceptives to girls under 16 without the parents' consent. The case went to appeal where it was upheld and it took a government appeal to the House of Lords to overturn it.

GPs appear to remain somewhat cautious about providing such services on a confidential basis. But the confidentiality issue is a key one which inhibits both professionals (and not just doctors) and their potential clients: this is discussed in the final chapter.

Bledin and MacPherson (1984) point out that 'little research has been directed at establishing what factors attract patients – and in particular young patients – to family planning clinics' (p. 29). In their study they interviewed 52 teenage abortion patients. They found that around half the girls did not know that such clinics were open to all. Younger girls in particular appeared to be deterred by ignorance of 'what happens' at such clinics and associated embarrassment. The authors concluded that there was a need to orientate such services towards younger women.

That study is more than ten years old but a recent review by Jacobson, Wilkinson and Pill (1995) on the provision of primary care in the UK indicates that teenagers are still generally apprehensive about consulting their GPs or para-medical professionals and they conclude that 'ideally the individual teenage girl should be allowed to make her own choices; and little is currently known about the sensitivities or wishes of the consumer' (p. 234).

IMPROVING THE SITUATION

It is ironic that the lead in developing information and clinic-based services for teenagers has been given by independent agencies of charitable status. The FPA's information service is remarkably comprehensive, but it is only the Brook Centres that provide a service for contraceptive advice and supplies specifically for young people: it is thinly spread. Local Health Boards provide family planning services but there is usually only very limited *specific* provision for teenagers.

Attempts to develop services in an innovative, collaborative fashion frequently run into difficulty in the face of ambivalence at various levels. A very carefully thought-out and developed project for service provision in Liverpool in the 1980s foundered in just this fashion (Ashton, 1989). In that area there is one of the highest teenage pregnancy and abortion rates in the UK, and the highest illegitimacy rate, along with Greater London.

In 1983, at the request of the Health Education Council, a pilot project was set up in order to develop a community-based service for young people. A wide process of consultation and agreement was established, but after three years' work the project was rejected by the commissioning authority without any clear reason.

Ashton refers to the climate of the time 'which included the Gillick affair, attempts . . . to restrict sex education in schools; Family Planning Information Service literature which included a diagram of an erect penis had to be destroyed; and there was generally a concerted effort to impose a particular view of morality on the nation's teenagers' (p. 50).

The moral ambivalence of this hardly needs underlining but itself needs to be understood. This social process is considered in the final chapter.

6

POLICY AND PRACTICE

GOVERNMENT POLICY

In its 1992 White Paper *The Health of the Nation*, the then UK government set a target for reducing the conception rate in girls under 16 by at least 50 per cent by the year 2000 from the 1989 figure of 9.5 per 1,000 girls aged 13–15 (Secretary of State for Health, 1992). There is a good case for targeting reduction on this age range because there is least argument about the rightness of it: most young women who report the experience of sexual intercourse before the age of 16, with hindsight, express the feeling that it was 'too soon' (Johnson *et al., op. cit.*). And it is clear from the high abortion rate at this age level that most of such pregnancies are unintended. This is not to say that they are always *unwanted* or to assume that the girls may not have been under some pressure to consent to an abortion.

In 1994 the number of under-16 conceptions in England and Wales (estimated by combining the number of births and abortions under 16 with two-thirds of births at age 16) was approximately 7,000 (GSS, 1996a, 1996b). This group has to be seen as relatively distinct because it is particularly vulnerable:

- because of their own (and their sexual partner's) knowledge that sexual intercourse at this age can be illegal;
- because there are barriers to confidentiality in their attempts to get help (both in their own minds and in the attitudes and practices of relevant professionals);
- because, for related reasons, they may have poor knowledge of contraceptive practice and limited access to advice and contraceptive supplies;
- because their social, economic and educational conditions give them limited power of independent action.

Conceptions in England and Wales for the same year, and estimated by the same formula, for those aged 16–19 amounted to around 80,000. If teenage pregnancy is a problem, then this is a much bigger one. But is it a problem, and, if so, in what respects?

WHAT IS THE PROBLEM?

Teenagers who conceive over the age of 16 do so as legal adults in relation to sexual behaviour and there is no question as to their right to medical confidentiality. That doesn't mean they feel confident in their dealings with GPs and other medical staff (see discussion in Jacobson, Wilkinson and Pill, 1995, p. 234). True, a high proportion of conceptions are terminated, but this is true at all ages (see Chapter 1).

Jacobson *et al.* (*op. cit.*) comment that 'While teenage pregnancy represents a problem for society, it is less apparent if it is a problem for the young women involved' (p. 233). Rhode (1994), Professor of Law at Stanford University, in a review of adolescent pregnancy and public policy points out that 'Much of the problem stems from disputes over the nature of the problem. Is the primary issue morality, fertility, or poverty?' (p. 635).

Is it wrong to have babies as a teenager? Teenagers are more likely to be poor and unmarried, but poor and unmarried women are having babies at *all* ages – indeed, the majority of such births occur to older women. Is it that teenagers get pregnant too easily or fail to use adequate forms of birth control? The evidence is that this age group is very birth control-conscious but is poorly served by the 'family planning' services, however provided. Whose fault is that? And contraceptive failure has a high rate at all ages – as the abortion statistics demonstrate. Is their relative poverty the problem? Would teenage pregnancies be acceptable if the mothers were economically self-sufficient and not a 'charge' on the state? If the answer to this is 'Yes' then the implication is that any poor parents should not have children because they too will require state subsidy. The deeper question is: who is responsible for poverty? – and who should do something about it?

Rhodes (*op. cit.*), speaking of the US situation, but with recognizable application to the UK, comments:

Too often, decision makers have located the problem at the individual level and faulted teens who want 'too much too soon' in sexual relationships. Insufficient attention has focused on the societal level, on structures that offer females 'too little too late': too little reason to stay in school, too little assistance in birth control, too little opportunity for childcare health services, vocational training or decent jobs, and too little understanding of the responsibilities of single parenthood. (p. 636)

Rhodes' rhetoric is echoed in the findings of the UK empirical study 'Teenage Mothers and Their Partners' by Simms and Smith (1986) previously cited. In their final discussion chapter 'Some consequences for social policy' they highlight the following issues:

- the lack of school sex education dealing with birth control;
- the lack of *practical* knowledge even in those girls who had received this 'educational' input;
- the obstruction by doctors experienced by some of the sample when they raised the issue of abortion (though there were also other pressures in their social and family circle);
- the rarity of social worker involvement even when there were severe social and marital problems;
- the boredom and isolation experienced by many young women and the need for day nurseries and social support for young mothers;
- the lack of autonomy;
- the desire expressed by many of them for part-time work (found in the Brown and Harris study to be an important factor in mental health).

The authors conclude that: 'It would not be difficult to transform the situation of most of these young mothers if enough resources were devoted to this. The question to be determined is what priority they have in relation to other needy groups in the community. This is an issue of policy, not research' (p. 104).

The job of research is to inform policy although it would be naïve in the extreme to assume any direct, rational process. Policy is not so simple.

THE MORAL OBJECTIONS TO TEENAGE PREGNANCY

Moral and political reaction, if it is informed at all, tends to be a response to headline summary statistics. And it is only 'scare' statistics that get reported. Dr Margaret Jones, Chief Executive of the Brook Advisory Centres, in the organization's Annual Report for 1995–96 (BAC, 1996a) comments: 'During 1995–96 we saw a drop in the teenage conception rate for the third successive year . . . this is good news, although as such it was conspicuous by its absence in the media!' (p. 1).

What is the *real* situation and experience of teenage mothers? What are their circumstances actually like? What are their wishes and aspirations?

Two qualitative studies in this area were published in 1995 by the Family Policy Studies Centre (Speak *et al.*, 1995; Burghes and Brown, 1995). In the latter study 31 teenage mothers were interviewed, 12 of whom were cohabiting or married. This is a small number but the findings are very clear:

> No matter how personally happy they were with their children, the young women took no great pride or pleasure in being lone parents. They had not planned to be young single mothers or, in most cases, to become pregnant so young. They . . . would have preferred . . . setting up home in an established relationship and not having their first child until their mid-twenties.
>
> . . . although they were not living with a partner when interviewed, a half of the single lone mothers had cohabited with the fathers of their children *at some time*. These relationships had . . . broken down . . . Policy-makers, in particular, should beware of treating the rise in single lone motherhood as if it were an entirely separate issue of young women having babies on their own. This is far from the case. (p. 60)

The same study highlights the external economic factors which impinge on young parents' poverty and that 'By 1994, only a half of teenage men and 7 out of 10 of those in their early twenties were in employment; one in five young men aged 16–19 and one in seven of those aged 20–29 were unemployed' (p. 61). Nor is employment necessarily the solution since wages for young people have fallen and those who, for one reason or another, are in 'further' education exist on limited, if any, grant support. The economic situation of these young men hardly permits financial responsibilities.

A common charge is that young women become pregnant to get preferential access to housing. This was not true of the young women in the study, but wider evidence is also against it. The authors point out that:

- most teenage conceptions are accidental;
- mothers under 18 are not usually allowed to put their names on local authority housing waiting lists;
- teenage mothers are not generally knowledgeable about access to housing;
- where teenage mothers are housed, it is not at the expense of two-parent families with children (p. 61);
- to this could be added the recent finding that 50 per cent of single mothers under 21 are still living with their parents (BAC, 1996a).

Burghes and Brown conclude that 'The question raised is how to help single lone mothers to develop and prosper (and their children likewise) as well as increase their self-sufficiency without creating perverse incentives for more young women to follow the same course' (p. 64).

There is little evidence that this would be the case, whereas there is good evidence that allowing young mothers and their children to live in poverty has devastating long-term results (Gillham, 1994, pp. 84–97).

THE POLITICS OF CHOICE

Taking punitive action against young women (or any other women) who *choose* to become pregnant is a moral stance so extreme as to be beyond the character of this book and outside the ethics of most professions. But it is apparent that many and *probably the majority* of teenagers do *not* choose to become pregnant. The humane and professional question is: what can we do to help them? What are the obstructions to helping them achieve the kind of life they want?

POVERTY AND SOCIAL DISADVANTAGE

Many of our social problems are endemic because poverty is endemic. If governments are limited in their ability to tackle this fundamental problem, it is idle for professional groups to think they can do so. But mitigating the effects of poverty in certain respects is another matter.

Medical researchers concerned with the epidemiology of teenage conceptions, e.g. Wilson, Brown and Richards (1992) commonly argue that: 'Reduction of social factors which precipitate teenage conception may have more impact than a reinvestment in traditional family planning services' (p. 23). Smith (1993) in the Tayside Study previously cited points out that: 'The wide geographical variation in patterns of teenage pregnancy indicates the need for a small area rather than a regional approach to setting targets and devising measures of achieving them' (p. 1232).

Poor educational achievement is characteristic of young teenage mothers and has to be taken account of in any assumption that employment is an attractive alternative to motherhood. Burghes and Brown, in their qualitative study of teenage mothers (*op. cit.*) comment on the 'gap between their aspirations and their general lack of qualifications, skills or work experience' (p. 64). Raising the standard of vocational education for young women in high-risk areas could be *part of* a preventive strategy. All the evidence points to the need for a multi-stranded approach involving co-operation between different agencies, public and voluntary, and different professions – medicine, nursing, psychology, education, social work – and targeted on priority areas.

IMPROVEMENT OF EDUCATIONAL STANDARDS AND EMPLOYMENT PROSPECTS FOR YOUNG PEOPLE

High unemployment rates amongst young people are an insufficiently recognized factor in the development of single-mother families. Teenage fathers who have a low income and poor job prospects are unlikely to be able to fulfil the role implicitly expected of them. Simms and Smith (1986) comment on how little researched and regarded teenage fathers are. The push towards 'further training' does not ease the problem because this also connotes low income and a 'dependent' status.

Educational attainments for the lowest quartile of this age group (where most teenage mothers and fathers are to be found) are low and, if anything, getting lower as surveys on literacy standards and the attainments of school leavers indicate (Ekinsmyth and Bynner, 1994; National Child Development Study, 1987; Gorman and Fernandes, 1992). *A focus on the basic educational skills of this group combined with vocational training and adequate financial support could have considerable impact on the problem.*

IMPROVING THE ADEQUACY OF SEX EDUCATION

This is not the place to repeat the conclusions of the review of sex education in Chapter 4 but to emphasize the severe constraints imposed on its effectiveness.

- Although sex education is *required* of state secondary schools and must include information on HIV and AIDS and other sexually transmitted diseases, *contraceptive* education is not a requirement.
- Teachers are not expected to give advice on contraception but may give advice on where such help can be obtained. They can do this even if the parents have withdrawn their child from the school's sex education classes *unless the school policy states otherwise*.
- Teachers are usually bound by rules of disclosure (to the head teacher and parents) but teachers and pupils are often unclear about this. However, this is a matter of *school policy* and Department for Education guidance on this is not legally binding (see Chapter 4).

Although this framework is restrictive it can be seen that *if clearly understood* it does not constitute a barrier to giving effective advice and education. However, professional confusion and uncertainty (even amongst doctors) is such that the Brook Advisory Centre has recently (1996b) published guidance on confidentiality and the under-16s under the title 'What Should I Do?'

The Brook Annual Report (*op. cit.*) comments:

Confidentiality is the cornerstone of all successful young people's services. Time and again research shows that teenagers, particularly under-16s, will not seek sexual health advice unless they are explicitly reassured that their visit will be confidential. Indeed for many the anxiety of a breach of confidentiality far outweighs the seemingly remote risk of pregnancy and often prolongs risk-taking in early sexual activity . . . 84% of under-16s think it would be helpful to talk to their teacher about contraception but 64% would not do so if their parents had to be told. (p. 5)

This last point underlines the great potential of schools for providing contraceptive advice because they are, for under-16s, a *universal* service.

IMPROVING CONFIDENCE IN GPS AND ACCESS TO CONTRACEPTIVE SERVICES

1995–96 saw a drop in the teenage conception rate for the third successive year. This has followed an increase in the provision of young people's services and increased use of them by young people. Brook reports that in 1995–96 12 per cent of clients were under 16, compared with 4 per cent five years previously (BAC, 1996a).

The same report emphasizes that:

One aspect of service provision which is sometimes overlooked by health authorities is the importance of providing and promoting clinics *specifically* for young people, rather than just relabelling existing family planning clinics. This is crucial for younger teenagers to whom the prospect of meeting mum or a family friend poses a far greater risk than the seemingly remote risk of pregnancy from unprotected sex. One of Brook's oldest branches, which had accumulated a sizeable proportion of older clients, saw a 40% increase in under-16s when they restricted some sessions to under-25s. (p. 1)

GPs in the UK NHS are the central figures in primary health care, including the provision of contraceptive services. Theoretically, teenagers simply need to visit their GP for assessment and advice. But, as most research attests (see review in Jacobson, Wilkinson and Pill, 1995) the relationship is not an easy or confident one, at least from the teenager's perspective. From the perspective of the GP the issue of confidentiality and the appropriateness of giving contraceptive advice can inhibit a helpful response. Following the Gillick case previously discussed, doctors in England and Wales are bound by the 'Fraser Guidelines' issued by Lord Fraser following the 1985 House of Lords ruling in that case. They have to be satisfied that *all* the following requirements are met (from BAC, 1996b):

- the young person understands the doctor's advice;
- the doctor cannot persuade the young person to inform his or her parents or allow the doctor to inform the parents that he or she is seeking contraceptive advice;
- the young person is very likely to begin or continue having sexual intercourse with or without contraceptive treatment;
- unless he or she receives contraceptive advice or treatment, the young person's physical or mental health or both are likely to suffer;
- the young person's best interests require the doctor to give contraceptive advice, treatment or both without parental consent.

The Medical Defence Union for doctors in Scotland gives essentially similar advice.

It is evident that these guidelines, resting as they do heavily on the doctor's judgement and opinions, could easily be interpreted negatively. However, guidance issued to GPs by the BMA (1993) emphasizes that:

- Many teenagers risk pregnancy rather than seek contraceptive advice.
- Many teenagers mistakenly fear that their GP cannot respect their confidentiality.
- The duty of confidentiality owed to a person under 16 is as great as that owed to any other person.
- Any competent young person, regardless of age, can independently seek medical advice and give valid consent to medical treatment. (p. 1)

What is significant is that the BMA, and related agencies, saw it as necessary to issue this advice to GPs so long after the Gillick case. And whilst the situation is undoubtedly improving, the scope for further improvement is very great.

MORAL AMBIVALENCE ABOUT ADOLESCENT SEXUALITY

The international review by Jones *et al.* (1986) identified this issue as the heart of the matter: the extraordinary dual standards that exist, particularly in the US, but in the UK as well. Whilst relatively explicit sex scenes can be shown on TV, as well as health education promotions on HIV infection and safer sex, advertisements specifically for contraceptives or contraceptive services cannot.

The great success of the Dutch in even further reducing teenage pregnancies (discussed in Chapter 4) is testimony to a culture where teenage sexuality (and sexuality in general) is treated far more openly. Reporting the findings presented to a recent conference, Jacobson, Wilkinson and Pill (1995) comment:

> The teenager and the doctor feel comfortable discussing sexuality in a warm, mutually supporting atmosphere. Requests for contraceptive services are not associated with shame or embarrassment. The media is willing to carry messages designed for young people about contraceptive services and educational policy based on the emotions of sexuality as well as the mechanics. (p. 235)

Whatever else we do, radical improvement is unlikely to come about until the fundamental attitude in the UK matches this. Policy and practice are built on the bedrock of society-wide attitudes and values.

REFERENCES

Allen, I. (1987) *Education in Sex and Personal Relationships.* London: Policy Studies Institute.

American Public Welfare Association (1986) *Issues and Actions: Dialogue from Wingspread.* Washington D.C.: APWA.

Ashton, J. (1989) The Liverpool project to reduce teenage pregnancy. *British Journal of Family Planning.* **15**, 46–51.

Babb, P. (1993) Teenage conceptions and fertility in England and Wales 1971–91. *Population Trends* (No. 74). London: HMSO.

Balding, J. (1994) *Young People in 1993.* University of Exeter: Schools Health Education Unit.

Battin, M. P. (1995) A better way of approaching adolescent pregnancy. *Social Science and Medicine*, **41**, 9, 1203–5.

Beard, R. (1981) Chapter in: D. F. Roberts and R. Chester (eds.), *Changing Patterns of Conception and Fertility.* London: Academic Press.

Berger, D. (1979) Child abuse simulating 'near miss' sudden infant death syndrome. *The Journal of Pediatrics*, **95**, 554–6.

Bledin, K. D. and MacPherson, M. B. A. (1984) Teenage abortion patients and NHS family planning clinics: A survey of knowledge and attitudes. *Journal of Biological Science*, **1**, 29–37.

British Market Research Bureau (1994) *Young People's Attitudes Towards Sex Education.* London: Family Planning Association.

British Medical Association (1993) *Confidentiality and People Under 16.* London: BMA.

Brook Advisory Centres (1996a) *Annual Report 1995–1996.* London: Brook Advisory Centres.

Brook Advisory Centres (1996b) *What Should I Do?* London: BAC.

Brown, G. W. and Harris, T. (1978) *Social Origins of Depression: A Study of Psychiatric Disorder in Women.* London: Tavistock.

Burghes, L. and Brown, M. (1995) *Single Lone Mothers: Problems, Prospects and Policies*. London: Family Policy Studies Centre.

Butler, N. R. and Golding, J. (eds.) (1986) *From Birth to Five : A Study of Health and Behaviour of Britain's Five Year Olds*. Oxford: Pergamon.

Carstairs, V. and Morris, R. (1991) *Deprivation and Health in Scotland*. Aberdeen: Aberdeen University Press.

Creighton, S. J. (1985) An epidemiological study of abused children and their families in the United Kingdom between 1977 and 1982. *Child Abuse and Neglect*, **9**, 441–8.

Creighton, S. J. (1992) *Child Abuse Trends in England and Wales, 1988–1990*. London: NSPCC.

Creighton, S. J. and Noyes, P. (1989) *Child Abuse Trends in England and Wales, 1983–1987*. London: NSPCC.

Davies, J. and Coggans, N. (1991) *The Facts About Adolescent Drug Abuse*. London: Cassell.

Dawson, D. A. (1986) The effects of sex education on adolescent behaviour. *Family Planning Perspectives*, **18**, 4, 162–70.

DFE (1994) *Education Act 1993: Sex Education in Schools* (Circular Number 5/94). London: Department for Education.

Department of Health (1996) *Children and Young People on Child Protection Registers Year Ending 31 March 1995*. London: Government Statistical Service.

Dunnell, K. (1979) *Family Formation 1976*. London: HMSO.

Edwards, L. E., Steinman, M. E., Arnold, K. A. and Hakanson, E. V. (1980) Adolescent pregnancy prevention services in high school clinics. *Family Planning Perspectives*, **12**, 16–24.

Ekinsmyth, C. and Bynner, J. (1994) *The Basic Skills of Young Adults*, London: Basic Skills Unit.

FPA (1995a) *FPA Factsheet 5c*: Young people and sex education. London: Family Planning Association.

FPA (1995b) *FPA Factsheet 5d*: Sex education in schools. London: Family Planning Association.

FPA (1996) *Annual Report 1995–1996*. London: Family Planning Association.

Family Policy Studies Centre (1995) *Families in Britain*, (Family Report 3). London: Family Policy Studies Centre.

Farber, E. A. and Egeland, B. (1987) Invulnerability among abused and neglected children. In: E. J. Anthony and B. J. Cohler (eds), *The Invulnerable Child*. New York: Guilford Press.

Farrell, C. (1978) *My Mother Said . . . The Way Young People Learned about Sex and Birth Control*. London: Routledge and Kegan Paul.

Fraser, A. M., Brockert, M. P. H. and Ward, R. H. (1995) Association of young maternal age with adverse reproductive outcomes. *The New England Journal of Medicine*, **332**, 17, 1113–17.

Garbarino, J. (1976) A preliminary study of some ecological correlates of child abuse: The impact of socioeconomic stress on mothers. *Child Development*, **47**, 178–85.

Gelles, R. J. (1989) Child abuse and violence in single-parent families: Parent absence and economic deprivation. *American Journal of Orthopsychiatry*, **59**, 4, 492–501.

GRO (1996) *Annual Report of the Registrar General for Scotland 1995*, Edinburgh: General Register Office.

Gillham, B. (1994) *Child Physical Abuse*. London: Cassell.

Gillham, B. and Thomson, J. (eds) (1996) *Child Safety: Problem and Prevention from Preschool to Adolescence* (Chapter 1). London: Routledge.

Gorman, T. and Fernandes, C. (1992) *Reading in Recession*. Slough: NFER.

GSS (1996a) *Abortion Statistics: England and Wales 1994*. London: HMSO.

GSS (1996b) *Birth Statistics: England and Wales 1994*. London: HMSO.

Gress-Wright, J. (1993) The contraception paradox. *The Public Interest* (Fall Issue), 15–25.

Hirsch, M. B., Zabin, L. S., Streatt, R. F. and Hardy, J. B. (1987) Users of reproductive health clinic services in a school pregnancy prevention program. *Public Health Reports*, **102**, 3, 307–16.

Holden, E. W., Willis, D. J. and Corcoran, M. M. (1992) Preventing child maltreatment during the prenatal/perinatal period. In:

Prevention of Child Maltreatment: Developmental and Ecological Perspectives. New York: John Wiley.

Howard, M. and Mitchell, M. E. (1993) Preventing teenage pregnancy: Some questions to be answered and some answers to be questioned. *Pediatric Annals*, **22**, 109–18.

Ingham, R. (1994) Some speculations on the concept of rationality. *Advances in Medical Sociology*, **4**, 89–111.

Ingham, R., Woodcock, A. and Stenner, K. (1991) Getting to know you . . . young people's knowledge of their partners at first intercourse. *Journal of Community and Applied Psychology*, **1**, 2, 117–32.

Jacobson, L. D., Wilkinson, C. and Pill, R. (1995) Teenage pregnancy in the United Kingdom in the 1990s: The implications for primary care. *Family Practice*, **12**, 2, 232–6.

Jason, J., Carpenter, M. M. and Tyler, C. W. (1983) Underrecording of infant homicide in the United States. *American Journal of Public Health*, **73**, 2, 195–7.

Johnson, A. M., Wadsworth, J., Wellings, K. and Field, J. (1994) *Sexual Attitudes and Lifestyles.* Oxford: Blackwell Scientific Publications.

Jones, E. F., Forrest, J. D., Goldman, N., Henshaw, S., Lincoln, R., Rasoff, J. I., Westoff, C. F. and Wulf, D. (1986) *Teenage Pregnancy in Industrialised Countries.* New Haven: Yale University Press.

Kinsey, A. C., Pomeroy, W. B. and Martin, C. E. (1948) *Sexual Behavior in the Human Male.* Philadelphia: W. B. Saunders.

Kinsey, A. C., Pomeroy, W. B., Martin, C. E. and Gebhard, P. H. (1953) *Sexual Behavior in the Human Female.* Philadelphia: W. B. Saunders.

Kirby, D. (1989) Research on effectiveness of sex education programmes. *Theory into Practice*, **28**, 165–71.

Loewenstein, G. and Furstenberg, F. (1991) Is teenage sexual beheaviour rational? *Journal of Applied Social Psychology*, **21**, 12, 957–86.

Macdonald, D. I. (1987) An approach to the problems of teenage pregnancy. *Public Health Reports*, **102**, 4, 377–85.

Miller, R. (1995) Preventing adolescent pregnancy and associated risks. *Canadian Family Physician*, **41**, 1525–31.

Mullinar, G. (1994) *Developing Sex Education in Schools : A Practical Guide*. London: Family Planning Association.

National Child Development Study (1987) *Literacy, Numeracy and Adults*. London: Basic Skills Unit.

National Foundation for Educational Research (1994) *Parents, Schools and Sex Education*. London: Health Education Authority.

Newlands, M. and Emery, J. L. (1991) Child abuse and cot deaths. *Child Abuse and Neglect*, **15**, 275–8.

ONS (1996a) *Abortion Statistics: England and Wales 1994* (Series AB No. 21). London: HMSO.

ONS (1996b) *Birth Statistics: England and Wales 1994* (Series FM1 No. 23). London: HMSO.

ONS (1996c) *Mortality Statistics: Childhood, Infant and Perinatal: England and Wales 1993 and 1994* (Series DH3 No. 27). London: The Stationery Office.

ONS (1996d) *Monitor: Population and Health: Sudden Infant Deaths: England and Wales: 1991–1995* (Series No. DH3 96/2). London: Publications Unit, ONS.

ONS (1996e) *Mortality Statistics: Cause: England and Wales 1993 (revised) and 1994*. London: HMSO.

OPCS (1994) *Mortality Statistics: Cause: England and Wales 1993*. London: HMSO.

OPCS (1995a) *Mortality Statistics Perinatal and Infant: Social and biological factors: England and Wales 1992*. London: HMSO.

OPCS (1995b) *General Household Survey 1993*. London: HMSO.

Paykel, E. S. (1991) Depression in women. *British Journal of Psychiatry*, *158* (suppl. 10), 22–9.

Pearson, V. A. H., Owen, M. R., Pereira Gray, D. J. and Marshall, M. H. (1995) Pregnant teenagers' knowledge and use of emergency contraception. *British Medical Journal*, **310**, 1644.

Pugh, E. J., Statham, R. and Jarvis, S. (1987) Cot deaths, stillbirths, and the probation service: A potentially recognisable at-risk group. *Archives of Disease in Childhood*, **62**, 146–7.

Rhode, D. L. (1994) Adolescent pregnancy and public policy. *Political Science Quarterly*, **108**, 4, 635–69.

Rudat, K. (1992) *Today's Young Adults: 16–19 Year Olds' Views On and Experience of Sex Education*. London: Health Education Authority.

Russel, J. (1988) Early teenage pregnancy. *Maternal and Child Health*, (February), 43–6.

Secretary of State for Health (1992) *The Health of the Nation*. London: HMSO.

Sex Education Forum (1994) *Positive Guidance on Sex and Relationships Education* (Forum Factsheet 3). London: National Children's Bureau.

Schofield, M. (1965) *The Sexual Behaviour of Young People*. London: Longman.

Shah, F., Zelnik, M. and Kantner, J. (1975) Unprotected intercourse among unwed teenagers. *Family Planning Perspectives*, **7**, 39–44.

Simms, M. and Smith, C. (1986) *Teenage Mothers and their Partners: A Survey in England and Wales* (Research Report No. 15, Institute for Social Studies in Medical Care). London: HMSO.

Smith, T. (1993) Influence of socio-economic factors on attaining targets for reducing teenage pregnancies. *British Medical Journal*, **306**, 1232–5.

Speak, S., Cameron, S., Woods, R. and Gilroy, R. (1995) *Young Single Mothers: Barriers to Independent Living*. London: Family Policy Studies Centre.

Stier, D. M., Leventhal, J. M., Berg, A. T., Johnson, L. and Mezger, J. (1993) Are children born to young mothers at increased risk of maltreatment? *Pediatrics*, **91**, 3, 642–8.

Tanner, J. M. (1962) *Growth at Adolescence* (2nd edition). Oxford: Blackwell.

Vincent, M. L., Clearie, A. F. and Schlucter, M. D. (1987) Reducing adolescent pregnancy through school and community-based education. *Journal of the American Medical Association*, **257**, 2382–6.

Whitlow, B. J., Desmond, N. and Hay, P. (1995) Women know little about emergency contraception, and men know less. *British Medical Journal*, **311**, 806.

Wilson, S. H., Brown, T. P. and Richards, R. G. (1992) Teenage conception and contraception in the English Regions. *Journal of Public Health Medicine*, **14**, 1, 17–25.

Wolkind, S. N. and Kruk, S. (1985) Teenage pregnancy and motherhood. *Journal of the Royal Society of Medicine*, **78**, 112–16.

Wynder, E. L. (1969) Epidemiology of carcinoma *in situ* of the cervix. *Obstetric and Gynecological Survey*, **24**, 697–711.

Zabin, L. S., Hirsch, M. B., Smith, S., Streatt, R. F. and Hardy, J. B. (1986) Adolescent pregnancy-prevention program. *Journal of Adolescent Health*, **7**, 77–87.

Zabin, Kantner and Zelnik (1979) Risk of adolescent pregnancy in the first months of intercourse. *Family Planning Perspectives*, **11**, 215–26.

APPENDIX A

**Useful addresses and telephone numbers.
Agencies concerned with parenthood, contraception,
and sex education.**

The main national information agencies are **The Family Planning Association,** the **Brook Advisory Centres,** and the four **UK Health Promotion Agencies. The Family Policy Studies Centre** is essentially a research body but very informative on key policy issues. **The Contraception Information Service** (CES) is the National Contraceptive Service in the UK and is run by the FPA in partnership with the Health Promotion Agencies. Brook also provides a clinic service specifically for young people. Local Health Boards provide family planning services (listed in the telephone directory) and these may have specific facilities for young people.

1. The Family Planning Association Head Office and centre for **Healthwise** (The FPA Book Service) is based at:

2–12 Pentonville Road, London N1 9FP
Tel: 0171 837 5432
Fax: 0171 837 3026

There are also regional offices in Glasgow, Cardiff, Belfast and Londonderry. The **Healthwise** catalogue lists a wide range of books, videos and sex education programmes, not just those published by the FPA.

2. Brook Advisory Centres
The national office is based at:

165 Grays Inn Road, London WC1X 8UD
Tel: 0171 713 9000 (general enquiries)
0171 833 8488 (professional enquiries and publications)
Fax: 0171 833 8182

There are also a number of helplines of 24-hour recorded information for teenagers:

Emergency contraception 0171 617 0801
Missed a period?   0171 617 0802
Abortion   0171 617 0803

Starting contraception	0171 617 0804
Pregnant and unsure?	0171 617 0805
Visiting a Brook Centre	0171 617 0806
Sexually transmitted diseases	0171 617 0807

3. UK Health Promotion Agencies

These have libraries, resource centres and information services; they are regionally based as follows:

England: Resources Adviser, Health Education Authority, Hamilton House, Mabledon Place, London, WC1H 9TX. Tel: 0171 383 3833.

Scotland: Health Promotion Library Scotland, The Priory, Canaan Lane, Edinburgh, EH10 4SG. Tel: 0345 125442.

Northern Ireland: Resources Centre, Health Promotion Agency for Northern Ireland, 18 Ormeau Avenue, Belfast, BT2 8HS. Tel: 01232 311611.

Wales: The Library, Health Promotion Wales, Ffynnon-las, Ty Glos Avenue, Cardiff, CF4 5DZ, Tel: 01222 752222.

4. The Contraceptive Information Service

This national service provides information to the general public and professional groups:

- The CES **Helpline** provides confidential information and advice on contraception, as well as details of local services. Helpline open Monday to Friday, 9am – 7pm on 0171 837 4044.
- **The Contraceptive Education Bulletin** is a quarterly journal for professionals (subscription enquiries on 0171 837 5432).
- CES **Factsheets** give the latest findings on key topics such as sex education, abortion and contraception (for current list ring 0171 837 5432).
- CES library and information centre. A major reference resource for books and journals. Reference lists and photocopies available. Tel: 0171 923 5228.
- Press and media service for journalists, etc. on 0171 923 5242.
- Contraceptive method leaflets for the public. Ring 0171 837 5432 for information and current price list.

5. Family Policy Studies Centre is based at:

231 Baker Street, London NW1 6XE
Tel: 0171 486 8179
Fax: 0171 224 3510

The FPSC is an independent centre for research and information. It publishes original research as well as reviews of research relating to policy, some of which relate to single and teenage mothers. It is supported by the Joseph Rowntree Foundation.

APPENDIX B

Recommended publications for professionals, parents, teenagers and children.

Publications starred (*) are available from **Healthwise**.

1. *Anne Szarewski and John Guillebaud (1994) *Contraception: A User's Handbook*, Oxford University Press.
   - Expert, authoritative, up-to-date, and clearly written. An essential reference book for teenagers and adults.

2. *Elizabeth Fenwick and Richard Walker (1994) *How Sex Works: A Book of Answers for Teenagers and Their Parents*, Dorling Kindersley.
   - Clearly and attractively presented – an easy introduction.

3. **Is Everybody Doing it? Your Guide to Contraception* (1995), Family Planning Association.
   - 16-page booklet for 13–17 year olds.

4. *Robie H. Harris (1995) *Let's Talk About Sex*, Walker Books.
   - Much-praised introductory book for 10 year olds upwards.

5. *Gill Mulliner (1994) *Developing Sex Education in Schools*, Family Planning Association.
   - A basic and indispensable text for schools.

6. *Gill Lenderyon (1993) *Primary School Workbook: Teaching Sex Education Within the National Curriculum*, Family Planning Association.
   - A practical approach to the uncertainties teachers experience in developing sex education at this level.

7. *Debby Klein and Tara Kaufmann (1996) *Unplanned Pregnancy: Making the Right Choice for You*, Thorsons.
   - Helpful and practical to young women in a situation where they are subject to many pressures.

8. *What Should I Do?* Guidance on confidentiality and under-16s for nurses, social workers, teachers and youth workers (1996), Brook Advisory Centres.
   - Excellent, clear summary of the legal and practical constraints and what *can* be done.

9. *Confidentiality and People Under 16* (1993), BMA.
   - A leaflet for doctors which makes the legal/professional situation clear and also emphasizes the importance of the GP's role. (Available from Brook.)

INDEX

abortion
  as a factor in birth rates 2, 3
  rates 3, 4, 50, 59
  services 8, 57
  and social class 8, 13
  and teenagers 3
adolescent sexual behaviour
  29
age
  and maternity 6
  of sexual partners 35, 36
attitudes to teenage pregnancy
  10, 60, 63

Baltimore Pregnancy Prevention
  Programme 46
behaviour change 42, 43
births to teenagers 1
birth
  rates 1
  registration 4
BMA 67, 68
Brook Centres 2, 50, 51, 52, 56,
  57, 62, 65, 66

child abuse and neglect 21, 22
Child Protection Registers 21
conception rates 1, 2, 3
conceptions
  and marital status 3
  to teenagers 2
confidentiality 41, 57, 65, 66, 67
contraceptive
  failure 37, 55
  services 8, 50ff, 65ff
  use 35, 36, 52ff
'cot death' 17, 18

depression 23, 24

Education Acts 39, 40, 41
educational attainment 64, 65
educational level and sexual
  behaviour 34
emergency contraception 37,
  55
employment issues 64
epidemiology 64
ethnic/religious groups and sexual behaviour 34, 35

family background of teenage
  mothers 13
FPA 39, 51, 56, 57
Family Policy Studies Centre 2
Fraser Guidelines 67

General Register Office Scotland 17
Gillick, Victoria 57, 58, 68

health education 42, 43
Health Education Authority 39
Health Education Council 58
HIV/AIDS infection 27, 38, 41
homicide 20
homosexuality 41

income and family structure 12
infant mortality rates 14, 15, 19
  and social class 15
ICD (Ninth Revision) 17
international comparisions 44,
  68
IUD 49, 50, 54

Kinsey Reports 28

Liverpool Project 57
Local Health Boards 57

marital status and infant mortality 15, 16, 19
marriage and maternity 4
maternities to teenagers 2
maternal age
  and child abuse 22, 23
  and infant mortality 16, 17, 19, 20
Medical Defence Union 67
medical risks in teenage pregnancies 14, 15
Minnesota Project 24

National Birth Control Council 51
National Curriculum 40
NSPCC 21
Norplant 49, 50, 54

Office for National Statistics 17
Office of Population Census and Surveys 17
oral contraception 32

policy issues 60ff
postponing sexual involvement 47
poverty and teenage/single parents 13, 22, 60, 64
pregnancy rates 44, 45, 59

rationality and sexual behaviour 43, 44

St Paul Project 46
schools and sex education 39ff

Scotland, birth rates 6
Secretary of State for Education 40
Secretary of State for Health 59
sex education 38ff, 61, 65
  evaluation 46, 47, 48
  programmes 41, 42
sexual abuse and exploitation 36
sexual behaviour 27, 28, 29, 36, 43, 44, 55
  and social class 33, 34
sexual intercourse, first experience 29ff, 53
sexual maturity 29
SIDS (Sudden Infant Death Syndrome) 17, 18, 19
  and child abuse 18
  and marital status 17
  and teenage maternities 20
single parents 4, 12, 21, 22, 63
social disadvantage 7, 9, 19, 26, 33, 59, 61, 64
social situation of teenage mothers 11, 61, 62, 63
social support 23, 24
South Caroline Programme 47
Stopes, Marie 51

teenage magazines 39, 40

under-age conceptions 59
'undetermined' infant deaths 17, 18, 20
unmarried mothers 4

value judgements about teenage pregnancy 10, 11

Wellcome Foundation 27
White Paper 59